# NORTH CAROLINA
# Notary Public
# Manual

North Carolina Department
of the Secretary of State

# North Carolina Department of the Secretary of State

EXECUTIVE

**Elaine F. Marshall**  North Carolina Secretary of State
**Rodney Maddox**  Chief Deputy
**Haley Haynes**  Deputy Secretary
**George Jeter**  Director of Communications

NOTARY PUBLIC DIVISION

**Ozie Stallworth**  Director, Notary Enforcement and e-Notarization
**Tina DuPree**  Director, Notary Commissioning

The North Carolina Department of the Secretary of State gratefully acknowledges the School of Government's assistance with the production of this manual.

# Contents

A Message from the Secretary of State . . . . . . . . . . . . . . . . . . vii

1

Getting Started . . . . . . . . . . . . . . . . . . . . . . . . . . . . . . . . . . . . . 1

Qualifications . . . . . . . . . . . . . . . . . . . . . . . . . . . . . . . . . . . . . . . 1

Term of Office and Jurisdiction—G.S. 10B-9 . . . . . . . . . . . . . . . 3

County of Commission and Filing the Oath of
  Office—G.S. 10B-5(c) and 18 NCAC 07B .0503 . . . . . . . . . . . 4

2

How to Become a Notary . . . . . . . . . . . . . . . . . . . . . . . . . . . . . 7

Taking the Required Educational Course of
  Study—G.S. 10B-8 . . . . . . . . . . . . . . . . . . . . . . . . . . . . . . . . . 7

Applying for a North Carolina Notary Public
  Commission—G.S. 10B-6 . . . . . . . . . . . . . . . . . . . . . . . . . . . . 8

Process for Re-commissioning—G.S. 10B-11 and
  18 NCAC 07B .0402 . . . . . . . . . . . . . . . . . . . . . . . . . . . . . . . 14

Public Information . . . . . . . . . . . . . . . . . . . . . . . . . . . . . . . . . . 16

Confidential Information . . . . . . . . . . . . . . . . . . . . . . . . . . . . . 16

3

Denials . . . . . . . . . . . . . . . . . . . . . . . . . . . . . . . . . . . . . . . . . . . 17

Reasons for Denial of a Notary Public Application for
  Commission—G.S. 10B-5(d) and 18 NCAC 07B .0902 . . . . . . . 17

Right to Appeal Procedures . . . . . . . . . . . . . . . . . . . . . . . . . . 19

## 4

### Definitions . . . . . . . . . . . . . . . . . . . . . . . . . . . . .21

Definitions—G.S. 10B-3 and 18 NCAC 07B .0102 . . . . . . . . . . . .21

## 5

### Notarization Explained in Eight Simple Steps . . . . . . . . . . .29

Step 1. Require the Personal Appearance of the Principal
Signer(s) of the Document . . . . . . . . . . . . . . . . . . . . . . . . . .30

Step 2. Positively Identify the Principal Signer(s) of the
Document . . . . . . . . . . . . . . . . . . . . . . . . . . . . . . . . . . .30

Step 3. Verify the Signature on the Document . . . . . . . . . . . . . .32

Step 4. Take the Acknowledgment or Administer the Oath
or Affirmation. . . . . . . . . . . . . . . . . . . . . . . . . . . . . . . .33

Step 5. Complete the Journal Entry . . . . . . . . . . . . . . . . . . . .34

Step 6. Complete the Notarial Certificate Language . . . . . . . . . .35

Step 7. Sign the Notarial Certificate . . . . . . . . . . . . . . . . . . . .35

Step 8. Affix the Official Notary Seal . . . . . . . . . . . . . . . . . . . .36

Additional Steps . . . . . . . . . . . . . . . . . . . . . . . . . . . . . . . .36

## 6

### Notarial Certificates Explained. . . . . . . . . . . . . . . . . . . . .37

Completing the Certificate Forms—G.S. 10B-40 . . . . . . . . . . . .37

Administration of Oaths—G.S. 11-2 . . . . . . . . . . . . . . . . . . . .46

Verification or Proof Certificate for a Subscribing Witness . . . . .48

Verification or Proof Certificate for a Non-subscribing
Witness. . . . . . . . . . . . . . . . . . . . . . . . . . . . . . . . . . . . .52

Restrictions on the Use of Proof of Execution Certificates . . . . .54

Notarial Certificates from Other Jurisdictions. . . . . . . . . . . . . .55

Statutory Certificates for Wills, Powers of Attorney, and
Living Wills. . . . . . . . . . . . . . . . . . . . . . . . . . . . . . . . . . .55

Representative or Fiduciary Capacities . . . . . . . . . . . . . . . . . .56

7

Special Circumstances. . . . . . . . . . . . . . . . . . . . . . . . . . . . . . . . 57
Unique Notarial Acts. . . . . . . . . . . . . . . . . . . . . . . . . . . . . . . . . 57
Signing Agents, Settlement Agents, Closing Agents, and
    Mobile Notaries. . . . . . . . . . . . . . . . . . . . . . . . . . . . . . . . . 62
Reasons to Refuse to Notarize a Document. . . . . . . . . . . . . . . . 63
Voter Absentee Application. . . . . . . . . . . . . . . . . . . . . . . . . . . 66
Division of Motor Vehicles Documentation . . . . . . . . . . . . . . . . 68

8

Notary Violations . . . . . . . . . . . . . . . . . . . . . . . . . . . . . . . . . . 71
Notary Public Act Enforcement—G.S. 10B-60. . . . . . . . . . . . . . 71
Illegal Practices in the Mortgage Industry. . . . . . . . . . . . . . . . . 74
Illegal Actions Involving "Sovereign Citizens". . . . . . . . . . . . . . 75
The Right to Refuse Service . . . . . . . . . . . . . . . . . . . . . . . . . . . 77
The Most Common Notary Violations. . . . . . . . . . . . . . . . . . . . 78
The Top 10 Notary Violations . . . . . . . . . . . . . . . . . . . . . . . . . 78
How to File a Complaint. . . . . . . . . . . . . . . . . . . . . . . . . . . . . . 79
Limitations on the Notary's Authority . . . . . . . . . . . . . . . . . . . . 82
Advertising Notary Public Services in a Language Other
    Than English . . . . . . . . . . . . . . . . . . . . . . . . . . . . . . . . . . . 82
Posting Fees in English . . . . . . . . . . . . . . . . . . . . . . . . . . . . . . 82
Certifying a True Copy or Notarizing or Authenticating a
    Photograph . . . . . . . . . . . . . . . . . . . . . . . . . . . . . . . . . . . . 83
Using the Notary's Official Seal as an Endorsement for
    Anything . . . . . . . . . . . . . . . . . . . . . . . . . . . . . . . . . . . . . . 83

9

Changes in Notary Status. . . . . . . . . . . . . . . . . . . . . . . . . . . . . 85
Change of Address—G.S. 10B-50 . . . . . . . . . . . . . . . . . . . . . . . 86
Change of Name—G.S. 10B-51 . . . . . . . . . . . . . . . . . . . . . . . . 86
Change of County—G.S. 10B-52 . . . . . . . . . . . . . . . . . . . . . . . 88
Change of Both Name and County—G.S. 10B-53 . . . . . . . . . . . 89

Additional Obligations of Notaries. . . . . . . . . . . . . . . . . . . . . . . . .89

Resignation—G.S. 10B-54 . . . . . . . . . . . . . . . . . . . . . . . . . . . . . . .90

Disposition of Seal—G.S. 10B-55 . . . . . . . . . . . . . . . . . . . . . . . . .90

Disposition of the Notary Journal. . . . . . . . . . . . . . . . . . . . . . . . .91


Appendix A: North Carolina General Statutes Chapter 10B,
 Article 1—Notary Public Act . . . . . . . . . . . . . . . . . . . . . . . . . . .93

Appendix B: North Carolina Administrative Code Title 18,
 Subchapter 7B—Notary Public Division . . . . . . . . . . . . . . . . .139

Appendix C: North Carolina Registers of Deeds Contact
 Information. . . . . . . . . . . . . . . . . . . . . . . . . . . . . . . . . . . . . . . . . .155

*State of North Carolina*
*Department of the Secretary of State*

ELAINE F. MARSHALL
SECRETARY OF STATE                                    January 2016

The office of notary public has a long and proud history in our society. For generations, notaries have served as the front line of defense against document fraud and attempts at forgery. The work that notaries public do is rarely glamorous, but it is so important that the highest courts in this nation routinely accept properly notarized documents as evidence in legal matters.

You, as someone beginning your education to become a notary public, or as a commissioned notary purchasing this new manual, are accepting the duty to safeguard your friends, family, coworkers, and the People of the Great State of North Carolina against those who would seek to profit from a fraudulent deed, sales contract, title, will, or other legal document.

This means that the office of notary public is indeed an important one, and one that is perhaps needed more than ever in this busy 21st Century where the pressure to complete business deals and legal work quickly is greater than it has ever been. Indeed, it has been suggested that if notaries public across this country were unable to perform their certifications for even two days in modern America, our economy would essentially grind to a stop. There are very few other duties where the same could be said.

I urge all of you who are about to begin your notary education to take the instruction to heart, to see it as the noble duty it truly is, and to keep this new 2016 edition of the *North Carolina Notary Public Manual* with you at all times. The practical instruction, tips, and best practices described in this book are essential tools you can use to become a notary whose reputation for doing things the right way is beyond reproach.

For those of you who are already commissioned notaries, this book serves as a legally required replacement to the previous edition of the manual that you have now. But, you should want this book as a replacement in any case because of the updated information it contains, including the section of the North Carolina Administrative Code for notaries that was not contained in the previous edition.

In closing, thank you for your interest and your commitment to becoming an upstanding notary public. North Carolina is known for having one of the finest notary programs in the nation. Let us all—notary student, notary public, educator, and regulator—do everything in our power to uphold that outstanding reputation for the millions of people across North Carolina depending on us when it comes time to sign their names on the most important documents of their lives.

Yours truly,

*Elaine F. Marshall*

Elaine F. Marshall

# 1
# Getting Started

Qualifications . . . . . . . . . . . . . . . . . . . . . . . . . . . . . . . . . . . . . . . 1

Term of Office and Jurisdiction—G.S. 10B-9 . . . . . . . . . . . . . . . . . .3

County of Commission and Filing the Oath of Office—
    G.S. 10B-5(c) and 18 NCAC 07B .0503 . . . . . . . . . . . . . . . . . . . .4

The statutory qualifications for becoming a notary public in North Carolina are contained in **Section 10B-5 of the North Carolina General Statutes (hereinafter G.S.) and in Article VI, Section 8, of the North Carolina Constitution.** It is important for an applicant to make sure that he or she meets all of the qualifications to obtain a notary public commission before investing time and money into applying to becoming a notary.

## Qualifications

As a public official, a notary public must meet the standards set by Article VI, Section 8, of the North Carolina Constitution. A notary public may not hold public office if he or she:

- Has been convicted of a felony under North Carolina or federal law.
- Has been convicted of a felony in another state that is also considered a felony under North Carolina law.

1

- Has been convicted of corruption or malpractice in any office.
- Has been removed from any office by impeachment.

All of these constitutional disqualifications prevent anyone from holding the office of notary public if his or her citizenship rights have not been restored in the manner prescribed by law. However, individuals who have been incarcerated or placed on probation are able to submit an application for consideration provided that 10 years have passed since the applicant's last day of prison, parole, or probation. G.S. 10B-5(d)(2).

Under G.S. 10B-5, applicants for notary public commissions must also meet the following requirements:

- Be at least 18 years of age or legally emancipated as defined in Article 35 of Chapter 7B of the General Statutes.
- Reside or have a regular place of work or business in North Carolina.
- Reside legally in the United States.
- Speak, read, and write the English language.
- Possess a high school diploma or equivalent.
- Pass the course of notary public instruction with a score of at least 80 percent on the final exam. The approved courses are currently taught through the North Carolina Community College System and a number of other colleges and universities. An applicant should contact his or her local community college, college, or university for availability, location, and costs of the notary public course. Members of the North Carolina State Bar are not required to take the mandatory notary public course.
- Purchase and keep as a reference the most recent manual approved by the Secretary of State that describes the duties and authority of traditional notaries public and electronic notaries public.

- Submit an application containing no significant mis-statement or omission of fact. The application form shall be provided by the Department of the Secretary of State and is available on the Department's website at www.sosnc.gov. The application for an initial appointment is also available at the register of deeds office in each county. Every application shall include the signature of the applicant written with pen and ink, and the signature shall be notarized by a person authorized to administer oaths.
- Pay a non-refundable fee of fifty dollars ($50).

## Term of Office and Jurisdiction—G.S. 10B-9

The commission term for a North Carolina notary public is five years and it expires at midnight on the eve of the expiration date. The notary commission becomes effective once the notary takes the oath of office at the register of deeds office in the county of commissioning. Upon taking the oath, the notary will receive a notarial commission certificate that contains an expiration date. The expiration date is significant in that the notary must include it on every notary certificate he or she executes. The expiration date may be included within the notary seal or it can be written on the certificate along with the notary's signature as a part of every notary act.

> A North Carolina notary has statewide jurisdiction and may perform notarial acts in all 100 counties of the state, not just in the county of the commission.

North Carolina notaries enjoy statewide jurisdiction. Their commission only authorizes them to perform notarial acts within the geographical boundaries of this state, not in other states or jurisdictions.

Documents that are destined for other states or foreign jurisdictions can be notarized by a North Carolina notary as long as the notarization takes place in North Carolina.

When notarizing documents drafted in other jurisdictions, care should be taken to ensure that the notarial certificate language is substantially similar to North Carolina statutory certificates and that it does not require the notary to perform acts that are not authorized by law.

## County of Commission and Filing the Oath of Office—G.S. 10B-5(c) and 18 NCAC 07B .0503

A notary is commissioned in the county where he or she resides. Pursuant to G.S. 10B-5(c), "The notary shall be commissioned in his or her county of residence, unless the notary is not a North Carolina resident, in which case he or she shall be commissioned in the county of his or her employment or business." If the notary resides outside the State of North Carolina but works in North Carolina and has a regular place of business in North Carolina, the notary may be commissioned in the county in which he or she works. The granting of a commission to a non-resident is contingent on the Department's verification of the applicant's employment in North Carolina.

Once the Secretary of State approves the application for the notary commission, the Department will send an "oath notification" letter to the appointee. The appointee will have 45 days from the "issue date" printed on the notification letter to go to the register of deeds office in the county of the appointee's residence to present satisfactory evidence of identification and take the oath of office. The registers of deeds currently charge $10 for administering the oath of office to notary appointees.

After administering the oath, the register of deeds will award the notary his or her commission certificate and notify the Department that the oath has been taken.

If the appointee does not appear before the register of deeds within 45 days of commissioning (that is, the issue date on the oath notification letter), the register of deeds will return the commission certificate to the Department, and the appointee will be required to reapply to obtain a new commission. If the appointee reapplies within one year of the granting of the commission, the Secretary of State may waive the educational requirements pursuant to G.S. 10B-11(c) and Title 18 North Carolina Administrative Code Rule 7B .0106.

> An appointee for a notary commission or re-commission must not perform notary acts until the oath of office has been taken. To do so is a Class 1 misdemeanor.

After the notary takes the oath of office, the register of deeds will record the notary's oath and the notary's signature either manually or electronically. The notary's name will be entered in the register of deed's record of notaries public or recorded in the register's real property records and indexed in the grantor field. The record will be kept in perpetuity and will contain the name and signature of the notary as commissioned, the date the oath of office was administered, and the date of any restriction, suspension, revocation, or resignation.

# 2
# How to Become a Notary

Taking the Required Educational Course of Study—G.S. 10B-8 . . 7

Applying for a North Carolina Notary Public Commission—
    G.S. 10B-6. . . . . . . . . . . . . . . . . . . . . . . . . . . . . . . . . . . . .8
       Statement of the Applicant's Personal Qualifications—G.S. 10B-7 . . .9
       Notarized Declaration—G.S. 10B-12 . . . . . . . . . . . . . . . . . . . . . .12

Process for Re-commissioning—G.S. 10B-11 and
    18 NCAC 07B .0402 . . . . . . . . . . . . . . . . . . . . . . . . . . . . . .14

Public Information. . . . . . . . . . . . . . . . . . . . . . . . . . . . . . . . . .16

Confidential Information . . . . . . . . . . . . . . . . . . . . . . . . . . . . . .16

## Taking the Required Educational Course of Study—G.S. 10B-8

An applicant for a North Carolina notary commission must successfully complete a minimum of six hours of notary public education before becoming eligible to apply for an initial notary commission. An applicant must present an acceptable form of identification (see the definition of *satisfactory evidence* of identification in Chapter 4) and the most recently approved edition of the *North Carolina Notary Public Manual* to the instructor in order to take the notary public course. Failure to present these items will result in the applicant being dismissed from the course.

Licensed members of the North Carolina State Bar are exempt from the education requirement. However, they are required to obtain the approved *North Carolina Notary Public Manual* and submit the application along with the $50 filing fee.

The notary public course is taught in authorized colleges and universities throughout the state and in all 58 colleges in the North Carolina Community College System. A schedule of the community college system course offerings may be viewed on their website at **www.nccommunitycolleges.edu**. The course of instruction includes general provisions, administrative rules and standards, commissioning and re-commissioning procedures, notarial powers and limitations, notarial signature and seal requirements, changes in status, enforcement, sanctions and remedies, common Division of Motor Vehicles (DMV) document procedures, and ethics. The cost of the notary public course is set by the individual institution and may vary from college to college.

An applicant must attend the entire six hours of the course and receive a score of at least 80 percent on the test to pass the course. The tests administered by the certified instructors are all approved by the Department of the Secretary of State.

## Applying for a North Carolina Notary Public Commission—G.S. 10B-6

The official notary public application can be obtained from the notary public instructor at the time of class or from a register of deeds office. It may also be downloaded from the Department's website. (To download and check on the most current applications available, go the Department's website at **www.sosnc.gov**, Notary Public section.) The application must be complete and free of errors when it is submitted to the Department for approval. If there are three or more blank spaces, the Department will deny the application and the applicant will need to submit a new application and fee. Applicants who fail to submit a complete application within three months of passing the notary course will be required to start the application process over, including re-taking the notary public class. The application fee of $50 must be submitted along with the notary application in order for the application to be processed.

## Statement of the Applicant's Personal Qualifications—G.S. 10B-7

A statement of the applicant's qualifications is requested in the application. The statement includes the following:

1. *The applicant's full legal name.* This will be the name on an applicant's birth certificate, Social Security card, driver's license, passport, or other official form of acceptable identification document.
2. *The name to be used for commissioning, excluding nicknames.* The name used on the notary commission must be a part of the full legal name. Nicknames or shortened versions of the applicant's legal name are not permissible. For example, William cannot use the nickname Bill, and Victoria cannot be shortened to Vicki. However, John Paul Jones may be commissioned as John Jones or even as Paul Jones since they are both full parts of the legal name. There is also a restriction on the use of initials in the commissioned name. Only one initial may be used in the commissioned name—either the initial of the first name or the initial of the middle name, but not both. For example, John Paul Jones may be commissioned in the name of J. Paul Jones or John P. Jones. No single initials without a full first or middle name are permitted.
3. *The applicant's date of birth.* An applicant must be at least 18 years of age or legally emancipated to be

eligible to apply for a notary commission in North Carolina.

4. *The mailing address for the applicant's residence, the street address for the applicant's residence, and the telephone number for the applicant's residence.* The mailing address may be a PO Box, but the application must also include the physical address of the applicant's residence. The telephone number may be a cell phone number. Residential addresses, phone numbers, and email addresses are kept private, but business addresses and phone numbers are made available to the public.

5. *The applicant's county of residence.* This will be the county in which the notary is commissioned, unless the applicant lives out of state and has a regular place of business in North Carolina. If this is the case, the applicant will be commissioned in the county in which his or her regular place of business is located. (See G.S. 10B-3(20); G.S. 10B-5(c).)

6. *The name of the applicant's employer, the street and mailing address for the applicant's employer, and the telephone number for the applicant's employer.* The employer's address must be complete and include the street number and zip code. This address, however, can be a PO Box. The county in which the business is located must also be included. If the applicant is unemployed, retired, a student, or self-employed, the corresponding box must be checked.

7. *The applicant's occupation.* The applicant must either indicate the applicant's occupation or check a box for unemployed, retired, student, or self-employed.

8. *The last four digits of the applicant's Social Security number.*

9. *The applicant's personal and business email addresses.*

10. *A declaration that the applicant is a citizen of the United States or proof of the applicant's legal residency*

*in this country.* If the applicant is not a citizen of the United States, the applicant must be able to prove permanent residency by producing a copy of a valid Permanent Resident Card, Form I-551, or other form of identification/documentation proving his or her legal residency in the United States.

11. *Proof of the applicant's successful completion of the six-hour notary public course.* The original signature and date of the notary public instructor must appear on all initial applications before they may be considered for approval. Although attorneys licensed to practice law in North Carolina are exempt from having to take the course, they are encouraged to do so. Attorneys are required to purchase and keep the most current notary public manual approved by the Department, as are all other applicants for notary commissioning and re-commissioning.

12. *A complete listing of any issuances, denials, revocations, suspensions, restrictions, and resignations of a notarial commission, professional license, or public office involving the applicant in this or any other state or nation.* If the applicant answers affirmatively to this question, the listing must be accompanied by the name and address of each licensing, commissioning, or appointing agency that effected the disciplinary action(s). The dates and reasons for each action must also be included. The Department considers these applications on a case-by-case basis but will not consider the issuance of any commission under these circumstances until five years have passed since the disciplinary action occurred and all conditions of the action have been met.

13. *A complete listing of any criminal convictions of the applicant, including any pleas of admission or nolo contendere, in this or any other state or nation.* If the

applicant answers affirmatively to this question, the application must be accompanied by the following:

- A certified copy of the criminal record from each county of residence, judgment, and a probation release letter, if applicable.
- A signed written explanation from the applicant of the conviction(s) that includes the date(s) and place(s) of arrest(s) or violation(s); the name of the court and court case number; the code section of the violation; a brief description of the offense; and the sentence imposed.
- The date of release from probation, parole, or incarceration must be included in the statement along with a copy of citizenship restoration for those with felony convictions.

14. *Three completed Certificates of Moral Character from three individuals who are not related to the applicant on the form approved by the Department.*

15. *A complete listing of any civil findings or admissions of fault or liability regarding the applicant's activities as a notary in this or any other state or nation.*

   **An application will be denied if the applicant answers yes and the requested information listed above is not provided.**

16. *A declaration that the applicant can speak, read, and write in the English language.* This declaration is a sworn or affirmed statement contained in the oath certificate at the bottom of the application.

## Notarized Declaration—G.S. 10B-12

The notary applicant is required to swear or affirm to the truthfulness of the statements made on the application before another individual authorized to administer oaths. The applicant will sign the application before another notary and either swear or affirm to the following statements:

"I, _____ (name of applicant), solemnly swear or affirm under penalty of perjury that the information in this application is true, complete, and correct; that I understand the official duties and responsibilities of a notary public in this State, as described in the statutes; that I can speak, read and write in the English language; and that I will perform to the best of my ability all notarial acts in accordance with the law."

_____
(signature of applicant)

This declaration is also on the application for re-commissioning.

**The applicant for an initial commission or the applicant for a re-commission must be notarized (a notary cannot notarize his or her own signature).**

The application must be sent to the Department within three months of successfully completing the notary public course. *If the applicant fails to submit the application within this period, he or she will have to re-take the course and start the process all over again.*

## Nine Steps to Becoming a North Carolina Notary Public

1. Register to take the notary public course at your local community college, college, or university.
2. Obtain a *North Carolina Notary Public Manual* from your local or community college bookstore. The manual may also be obtained from the UNC School of Government's online bookstore at **www.sog.unc.edu/publications** or by calling 919.966.4119.

3. Take the notary public course and pass the notary public examination with a score of 80 percent or better.
4. Complete the notary public application and obtain your notary instructor's signature after successful completion of the notary public course.
5. Have the notary application notarized.
6. Send the notarized application along with a $50 registration fee to:

    North Carolina Department of the Secretary of State
    PO Box 29626
    Raleigh, NC 27626

7. Obtain the notary oath notification letter from the Department of the Secretary of State.
8. Take your oath at the register of deeds office in your county of residence within 45 days of the notary commission issue date. The register of deeds' fee for taking the oath will be $10.
9. Purchase a North Carolina notary seal.

## Process for Re-commissioning—G.S. 10B-11 and 18 NCAC 07B .0402

The notary may start the re-commissioning process 10 weeks prior to his or her commission expiration date. The fee for the re-commissioning application is $50. The process for re-commissioning is basically the same as for the initial commission. The major difference is that applicants for re-commission must take an online examination rather than the six-hour course of instruction that is required for first time applicants. However, if the notary's commission has been expired for more than one year, the applicant will be required to attend the six-hour notary public course pursuant to G.S. 10B-8(a).

A passing score of at least 80 percent is required for the online re-commissioning test. The applicant is allotted 30 minutes to successfully complete the online exam. The re-commissioning applicant can access the exam by going to the Department's website at **www.sosnc.gov** and navigating to the Notary Public home page. The applicant has three chances to pass the exam within 30 days of the first attempt. If the applicant fails the third and final exam, he or she is required to go back to a notary public course and successfully complete that six-hour course with at least an 80 percent on the final written exam.

If the notary is a licensed member of the North Carolina State Bar or if the notary has been continuously commissioned in North Carolina since July 10, 1991, and has never been disciplined by the Secretary of State, the notary is exempt from taking the online re-commissioning exam. These exempt individuals may obtain the form for re-commissioning through the **Online Reappointment** process on the Department's Notary Public website, from the **Forms** section of that website, or from a register of deeds office.

Upon the Secretary of State's approval of the re-commissioning application, the Department will send the appointee an "oath notification" letter to take to the register of deeds in the commissioning county in order to take an oath or affirmation for the new commission. The remaining steps are the same as those for the process for obtaining the initial notary commission. The notary's term of office is for another five years.

## Public Information

Because a notary public is a public officer of the state, certain information from his or her notary public application is readily available to the public, including the following:

1. Full legal name
2. County of commission
3. Employer's name
4. Employer's street and mailing addresses
5. Employer's phone number
6. Status of commission
7. Disciplinary action, if any

## Confidential Information

The notary's home address, email address, home phone number, Social Security number, and date of birth are considered confidential. This information will not be released unless the Department receives one of the following in writing: a subpoena, a court order, specific authorization from the notary, a statement of authority from law enforcement or a government agency, or a North Carolina State Bar applicant "Release of Information" form. 18 NCAC 07B .1001.

# 3
# Denials

Reasons for Denial of a Notary Public Application for
  Commission—G.S. 10B-5(d) and 18 NCAC 07B .0902 . . . . . . . 17
Right to Appeal Procedures. . . . . . . . . . . . . . . . . . . . . . . . . . . . . . 19

## Reasons for Denial of a Notary Public Application for Commission—G.S. 10B-5(d) and 18 NCAC 07B .0902

The Department of the Secretary of State may deny applications for commission as a notary public for the following reasons:

- An applicant's submission of an incomplete application or an application containing material misstatement or omission of fact.
- An applicant's conviction or plea of admission or nolo contendere to a felony or any crime involving dishonesty or moral turpitude. Crimes of dishonesty and moral turpitude include arson, assault, battery, child molestation, rape, child pornography, domestic violence, unlawful possession or sale of drugs, embezzlement, failure to pay child support, fraud, identity theft, and many other crimes. For an exhaustive list, see 18 NCAC 07B .0201. In no case may a commission be issued to an applicant

within 10 years after release from prison, probation, or parole, whichever is later. Applicants with questions about their eligibility should contact the Notary Enforcement Division prior to submitting an application to the Department.

- A finding or admission of liability against the applicant in a civil lawsuit based on the applicant's deceit.
- The revocation, suspension, restriction, or denial of a notarial commission or professional license by this or any other state or nation. In no case may a commission be issued to an applicant within five years after the completion of all conditions of any disciplinary order.
- A finding that the applicant has engaged in official misconduct, whether or not disciplinary action resulted.
- An applicant knowingly using or having used false or misleading advertising in which the applicant as a notary public represented powers, duties, rights, or privileges that the applicant did not possess by law.
- A finding by a state bar or court that the applicant has engaged in the unauthorized practice of law.
- An applicant being under a current disciplinary action by the Department, such as a period of suspension or revocation of a commission previously held by the applicant.
- An applicant's submission of an application with false information about the applicant's criminal record or record of civil lawsuit findings or admissions of liability based on the applicant's deceit.
- An applicant having notarized his or her own signature on the notary public application.
- Revocation, suspension, restriction, or denial of an applicant's other professional licenses by North Carolina or another state or nation.

Any criminal record resulting from convictions for misdemeanors, felonies, or crimes involving dishonesty or moral turpitude may result in the denial of a notary public commission. Although each application is judged on its own merits, applicants with such issues are less likely to be granted the privilege of being a notary public for the state of North Carolina.

## Right to Appeal Procedures

Applicants for commissioning or re-commissioning whose applications have been denied and those who have been disciplined by the Department have the right to file a petition for a contested case hearing. The petition form can be obtained by contacting the Office of Administrative Hearings by phone at 919.431.3000, by fax at 919.431.3100, or from their website at www.ncoah.com. There is generally a filing fee to file a petition for a contested case hearing, which is the equivalent of filing a lawsuit against the Department of the Secretary of State, to contest the decision to deny, suspend, or revoke a notary public commission. 18 NCAC 07B .0907.

Applicants have 60 days from the date of the Department's decision to file a petition for a contested hearing. The petition must be filed with the North Carolina Office of Administrative Hearings at one of the following addresses:

6714 Mail Service Center
Raleigh, NC 27699-6700

1711 New Hope Church Road
Raleigh, NC 27609

A copy of the petition filed with the Office of Administrative Hearings must also be served on the process agent for the Department of the Secretary of State at the following address:

North Carolina Department of the Secretary of State
Attn: General Counsel
PO Box 29622
Raleigh, NC 27626-0622

# 4
# Definitions

Definitions—G.S. 10B-3 and 18 NCAC 07B .0102 . . . . . . . . . . . . . 21

## Definitions—G.S. 10B-3 and 18 NCAC 07B .0102

It is critical for notary applicants to have a thorough understanding of the terms used in notary law. Many of these terms have been defined to make sure that notaries know what their responsibilities are in fulfilling their duties as officers of the state. The following definitions, found in the statute and regulations and used by the Department of the Secretary of State in this book, must be studied and understood to comprehend the responsibilities of notaries public as outlined in the Notary Act.

**Acknowledgment.**—A notarial act in which a notary certifies that at a single time and place all of the following occurred:

    a. An individual appeared in person before the notary and presented a record.
    b. The individual was personally known to the notary or identified by the notary through satisfactory evidence.
    c. The individual did either of the following:
        i.  Indicated to the notary that the signature on the record was the individual's signature.

ii. Signed the record while in the physical presence of the notary and while being personally observed signing the record by the notary. G.S. 10B-3(1).

**Applicant.**—An individual who seeks appointment or reappointment to the office of notary public. 18 NCAC 07B .0102(b)(1).

**Appoint or Appointment.**—The naming of an individual to the office of notary public after determination that the individual has complied with Chapter 10B of the General Statutes and Subchapter 07B of the Administrative Rules. The terms "appoint," "reappoint," "appointment," "reappointment," "commission," "recommission," "commissioning," and "recommissioning" all refer to the term "commission" as defined in G.S. 10B-3(4) or to the process of acquiring or maintaining such commission. 18 NCAC 07B .0102(b)(2).

**Appointee.**—An individual who has been appointed or reappointed to the office of notary public but has not yet taken the oath of office to be commissioned. 18 NCAC 07B .0102(b)(3).

**Affirmation.**—A notarial act which is legally equivalent to an oath and in which a notary certifies that at a single time and place all of the following occurred:

a. An individual appeared in person before the notary.
b. The individual was personally known to the notary or identified by the notary through satisfactory evidence.
c. The individual made a vow of truthfulness on penalty of perjury, based on personal honor and without invoking a deity or using any form of the word "swear." G.S. 10B-3(2).

**Attest or attestation.**—The completion of a certificate by a notary who has performed a notarial act. G.S. 10B-3(3).

**Commission.**—The empowerment to perform notarial acts and the written evidence of authority to perform those acts. G.S. 10B-3(4).

**Commissioning date.**—The date of commissioning or recommissioning as entered on a commission certificate. 18 NCAC 07B .0102(b)(4).

**Credible witness.**—An individual who is personally known to the notary and to whom all of the following also apply:

a. The notary believes the individual to be honest and reliable for the purpose of confirming to the notary the identity of another individual.
b. The notary believes the individual is not a party to or beneficiary of the transaction. G.S. 10B-3(5).

**Crime.**—A crime or:

a. Attempt to commit a crime;
b. Accessory to commission of a crime;
c. Aiding and abetting of a crime;
d. Conspiracy to commit a crime; or
e. Solicitation to commit a crime.

18 NCAC 07B .0102(b)(5).

**Department.**—The North Carolina Department of the Secretary of State. G.S. 10B-3(6).

**Director.**—The Division Director for the North Carolina Department of the Secretary of State Notary Public Section. G.S. 10B-3(7).

**Division.**—The Notary Public Section of the North Carolina Department of the Secretary of State. 18 NCAC .0102(b)(6).

**Jurat.**—A notary's certificate evidencing the administration of an oath or affirmation. G.S. 10B-3(8).

**Moral turpitude.**—Conduct contrary to expected standards of honesty, morality, or integrity. G.S. 10B-3(9).

**Nickname.**—A descriptive, familiar, or shortened form of a proper name. G.S. 10B-3(10).

**Notarial act, notary act, and notarization.**—The act of taking an acknowledgment, taking a verification or proof, or administering an oath or affirmation that a notary is empowered to perform under G.S. 10B-20(a). G.S. 10B-3(11).

**Notarial certificate and certificate.**—The portion of a notarized record that is completed by the notary, bears the notary's signature and seal, and states the facts attested by the notary in a particular notarization. G.S. 10B-3(12).

**Notary public and notary.**—A person commissioned to perform notarial acts under G.S. Chapter 10B. A notary is a public officer of the State of North Carolina and shall act in full and strict compliance with this act. G.S. 10B-3(13).

**Oath.**—A notarial act which is legally equivalent to an affirmation and in which a notary certifies that at a single time and place all of the following occurred:

a. An individual appeared in person before the notary.
b. The individual was personally known to the notary or identified by the notary through satisfactory evidence.
c. The individual made a vow of truthfulness on penalty of perjury while invoking a deity or using any form of the word "swear." G.S. 10B-3(14).

**Official misconduct.**—Either of the following:

a. A notary's performance of a prohibited act or failure to perform a mandated act set forth in G.S. Chapter 10B or any other law in connection with notarization.

b. A notary's performance of a notarial act in a manner found by the Secretary to be negligent or against the public interest. G.S. 10B-3(15).

**Personal appearance and appear in person before a notary.**—An individual and a notary are in close physical proximity to one another so that they may freely see and communicate with one another and exchange records back and forth during the notarization process. G.S. 10B-3(16).

**Personal knowledge or personally know.**—Familiarity with an individual resulting from interactions with that individual over a period of time sufficient to eliminate every reasonable doubt that the individual has the identity claimed. G.S. 10B-3(17).

**Principal.**—One of the following:

a. In the case of an acknowledgment, the individual whose identity and due execution of a record is being certified by the notary.
b. In the case of a verification or proof, the individual other than a subscribing witness, whose:
   i.  Identity and due execution of the record is being proven; or
   ii. Signature is being identified as genuine.
c. In the case of an oath or affirmation, the individual who makes a vow of truthfulness on penalty of perjury. G.S. 10B-3(18).

**Record.**—Information that is inscribed on a tangible medium and called a traditional or paper record. G.S. 10B-3(19).

**Regular place of work or business.**—A location, office, or other workspace, where an individual regularly spends all or part of the individual's work time. G.S. 10B-3(20).

**Revocation.**—The cancellation of the notary's commission stated in the order of revocation. G.S. 10B-3(21).

**Satisfactory evidence.**—Identification of an individual based on either of the following:

a. At least one current document issued by a federal, state, or federal or state-recognized tribal government agency bearing the photographic image of the individual's face and either the signature or a physical description of the individual.

b. The oath or affirmation of one credible witness who personally knows the individual seeking to be identified. G.S. 10B-3(22).

*Note:* The notary must be aware of additional information regarding the use of a *tribal identification (ID) card.*

A state statute, G.S. 143B-407, recognizes the following tribal governments:

- Coharie of Sampson and Harnett counties
- Eastern Band of Cherokees
- Haliwa-Saponi Tribe of Halifax, Warren, and adjoining counties
- Lumbees of Robeson, Hoke, and Scotland counties
- Meherrin of Hertford County
- Waccamaw-Siouan Tribe from Columbus and Bladen counties
- The Sappony
- Occaneechi Band of the Saponi Nation of Alamance and Orange counties
- Native Americans located in Cumberland, Guilford, Johnston, Mecklenburg, Orange, and Wake counties

Recognition of any other tribal government must be based on another state law or federal law.

Tribal cards should have at a minimum the following personal information:

- Name
- Photograph
- Tribal seal
- Tribal enrollment number
- Date of birth
- Name of mother and father
- Signature of cardholder or physical description
- Official signature of tribal chief

Some IDs may have pictures and physical descriptions, but it is up to the particular tribe. The notary must make sure that the ID has a photo and signature or physical description of the cardholder to satisfy the definition of "satisfactory evidence" of identity, above. It is also important to make sure that the tribal ID is from a legitimate state and federally recognized tribe.

Notaries may not rely on Matricula Consular Cards issued by a Mexican consulate as satisfactory evidence because they are issued by a consulate office and not through a centralized federal government database able to track them. The North Carolina Secretary of State therefore does not consider them to be issued by a federal government agency.

**Seal or stamp.**—A device for affixing on a paper record an image containing a notary's name, the words "notary public," and other information as required in G.S. 10B-37. G.S. 10B-3(23).

**Secretary.**—The North Carolina Secretary of State or the Secretary's designee. G.S. 10B-3(24).

**Subscribing witness.**—A person who signs a record for the purpose of being a witness to the principal's execution of the record or to the principal's acknowledgment of his or her execution of the record. A subscribing witness may give proof of the execution of the record as provided in the definition of "verification or proof," below. G.S. 10B-3(26).

**Suspension and restriction.**—The termination of a notary's commission for a period of time stated in an order of restriction or suspension. The terms "restriction" or "suspension" or a combination of both terms shall be used synonymously. G.S. 10B-3(27).

**Verification or proof.**—A notarial act in which a notary certifies that all of the following occurred:

a. An individual appeared in person before the notary.
b. The individual was personally known to the notary or identified by the notary through satisfactory evidence.
c. The individual was not a party to or beneficiary of the transaction.
d. The individual took an oath or gave an affirmation and testified to one of the following:
   i. The individual is a subscribing witness and the principal who signed the record did so while being personally observed by the subscribing witness.
   ii. The individual is a subscribing witness and the principal who signed the record acknowledged his or her signature to the subscribing witness.
   iii. The individual recognized either the signature on the record of the principal or the signature on the record of the subscribing witness and the signature was genuine. G.S. 10B-3(28).

# 5
# Notarization Explained in Eight Simple Steps

Step 1. Require the Personal Appearance of the Principal
Signer(s) of the Document . . . . . . . . . . . . . . . . . . . . . . . . . . . . .30

Step 2. Positively Identify the Principal Signer(s) of the
Document . . . . . . . . . . . . . . . . . . . . . . . . . . . . . . . . . . . . . . .30

Step 3. Verify the Signature on the Document . . . . . . . . . . . . . .32

Step 4. Take the Acknowledgment or Administer the Oath
or Affirmation. . . . . . . . . . . . . . . . . . . . . . . . . . . . . . . . . . . . . .33

Step 5. Complete the Journal Entry . . . . . . . . . . . . . . . . . . . . . . .34

Step 6. Complete the Notarial Certificate Language . . . . . . . . . .35

Step 7. Sign the Notarial Certificate . . . . . . . . . . . . . . . . . . . . . . .35

Step 8. Affix the Official Notary Seal . . . . . . . . . . . . . . . . . . . . . .36

Additional Steps . . . . . . . . . . . . . . . . . . . . . . . . . . . . . . . . . . . . .36

A notary public is an officer of the State of North Carolina. The signature and seal of a notary public, properly affixed to a certificate, represents that the notary executed the notarial act in compliance with North Carolina law. The notarial act and the steps to accomplish it are designed, in part, to enhance interstate recognition of notarial acts performed in North Carolina.

Because of the importance of the notarial act, the notary seal is the personal property of the notary and may never be used by anyone else. In fact, the law stipulates that the notary seal must be kept in a secure location and that an employer must surrender the seal to the notary upon termination of employment, regardless of who purchased the seal. G.S. 10B-36(a).

While the notarial act is not highly complex, there is certainly more involved with the process than simply "stamping and signing." There are no fewer than eight steps that must be taken to execute a proper notarization.

Depending on the type of notarization, the circumstances surrounding the identification of the principal signer(s), and the implementation of notarial best practices, there can be as many as nine steps to performing a proper notarization.

## Step 1. Require the Personal Appearance of the Principal Signer(s) of the Document

Personal appearance of the principal signer is required for any notarial act. This simply means that when the notary act occurs, the person requesting the notarization must appear before the notary with the document or record.

G.S. 10B-20(c)(1) states that a notary may not perform a notarial act if the principal or subscribing witness is not in the presence of the notary. A notary found guilty of performing a notarial act without requiring personal appearance may be charged with a Class 1 misdemeanor, G.S. 10B-60(c), or with a Class I felony if it is found that the notary intended to commit fraud. G.S. 10B-60(d).

## Step 2. Positively Identify the Principal Signer(s) of the Document

Each person requesting a notarization must be positively identified through either personal knowledge or satisfactory evidence of identity.

In order to rely on personal knowledge, the notary must be certain of a person's identity. The statute defines *personal knowledge* as "familiarity with an individual resulting from interactions with that individual over a period of time sufficient to eliminate every reasonable doubt that the individual has the identity claimed." G.S. 10B-3(17). A classic example would be two individuals who grew up together in the same neighborhood and had close interactions throughout the years as they attended the same school and the same place of worship for most of their lives.

If a notary has the slightest doubt about whether a signer is personally known, he or she must rely on another form of identification, referred to in the Notary Act as "satisfactory evidence." *Satisfactory evidence* is defined as a current state or federally issued identification (ID) card with a photograph and a physical description or signature. Identification cards issued by recognized state tribal agencies that meet these specifications are also acceptable.

The most common forms of identification are state driver's licenses, passports, and older military ID cards. The most recently issued military ID cards may generally not be used as "satisfactory evidence" of identity because the signature and physical description are embedded in a computer chip not visible to the naked eye.

If a signer is not personally known to the notary and does not possess an acceptable form of identification, there is another option. A mutual friend of the signer and the notary may act as a credible witness to confirm the identity of the signer. The mutual friend must be personally known to the notary; deemed by the notary to be honest, reliable, and impartial; and not a party to or a beneficiary of the transaction. G.S. 10B-3(5). Note that there is an additional step that must be followed for the credible witness (see the discussion below under "Additional Steps").

Given the high incidence of identity theft, mortgage fraud, and various other crimes in which imposters wreak havoc on society and on individual lives, it is critical for notaries to take their responsibility of positively identifying every document signer very seriously.

Notaries are prohibited from notarizing for a signer who has not been positively identified. Failure to comply with this mandate can result in a notary's commission being suspended or revoked. G.S. 10B-20(c)(2); G.S. 10B-60(a), (c).

## Step 3. Verify the Signature on the Document

The act of notarization centers around the signature of the principal signer(s). After all, it is the signature to which the notary is attesting. The document may or may not be signed in the presence of the notary when he or she is performing an acknowledgment. If the document has already been signed, the signer must indicate or acknowledge to the notary that he or she signed the document and did so willingly. G.S. 10B-3(1).

If an oath or affirmation is the notarial act being performed, the signer must always sign the document in the presence of the notary. This is because the jurat wording associated with an oath or affirmation states that the document was signed and sworn to before the notary. If the document has already been signed, the signer will need to sign it again before the notary so that the notary can make a proper attestation. Failure to have the signing occur in the presence of the notary is official misconduct for which the notary could be sanctioned.

In no circumstance may a notary perform a notarial act if there is no signature on the record. A mark can be a signature, as described in Chapter 7. G.S. 10B-20(d).

# Step 4. Take the Acknowledgment or Administer the Oath or Affirmation

The most common types of notarial acts are acknowledgments and oaths, which have two distinct functions.

When a notary is executing an acknowledgment, it is the principal signer who must acknowledge to the notary that the signature is indeed his or hers. If the document was signed previously, the notary must ask the signer of the record to acknowledge that the signature is his or hers and that the document was signed willingly. G.S. 10B-40(a1). Documents that are signed in the notary's presence do not require such discourse because the notary's firsthand account of the signing is a tacit acknowledgment and needs no further confirmation.

When a notary is administering an oath or affirmation, the notary must literally and physically administer the oath or affirmation. An oath is typically administered by having the signer raise his or her right hand toward the heavens, place his or her left hand on a holy book, and swear before God that the statements in the document are true and correct to the best of his or her knowledge. G.S. 10B-43. An affirmation is the legal equivalent of an oath and is given in the same manner, albeit without any reference to a supreme being or use of the word "swear." The typical wording is, "Do you affirm that the statements in this document are true?" A response in the affirmative is sufficient for the notary to complete the attestation.

When a notary is administering either an oath or an affirmation, the document being notarized must be signed in the presence of the notary. This requirement is dictated by the certificate wording for an oath or affirmation, which will state that the document was signed before the notary public.

## Step 5. Complete the Journal Entry

G.S. 10B-2(1)(3) states that the Notary Act's underlying purpose is "[t]o promote, serve and protect the public interest" and "[t]o prevent fraud and forgery." Maintaining a notary journal is in keeping with the purpose of the notary law in that it:

1. Causes would-be criminals to think twice before presenting a forged signature to a notary knowing that they will be asked to leave proof of their request in the form of their signature in a journal.
2. Provides a level of protection for the notary in the event that a signer later tries to disown a signature by providing clear evidence in the form of the person's signature that he or she did appear before a notary on a given date to request a notarization.
3. Provides valuable evidence to law enforcement officials investigating allegations of notary misconduct and criminal activity related to many forms of document fraud.

Given that the simple act of maintaining a notary journal is clearly in keeping with the stated purpose of the Notary Act, every notary should keep a chronological journal record of every notarial act to protect the notary, the public, and the integrity of the transaction.

Typical journal entries include the date and time of the transaction, the name(s) and signature(s) of the principal signer(s), the type of identification used to positively identify the signer(s), the type of document notarized, and the type of notarization that was performed. ~~Driver's license numbers~~ and ~~Social Security numbers should not be recorded in a notary journal.~~

# Step 6. Complete the Notarial Certificate Language

After taking the signer's acknowledgment or administering an oath or affirmation, the notary must complete a notarial certificate attesting to the facts of the notarial act.

In the case of an acknowledgment, the notary will complete a certificate that must contain the state and county where the notarial act took place, the name of the person whose signature is being acknowledged, the date of the acknowledgment, the legible appearance of the notary's name typed or printed, and a statement indicating that the signer acknowledged his or her signature to the notary. G.S. 10B-20; G.S. 10B-40(b).

For a jurat certificate that evidences the administration of an oath or affirmation, the notary will need to complete the certificate indicating that the signer signed in his or her presence and took either an oath or an affirmation swearing or affirming that the statements in the document are true. G.S. 10B-20; G.S. 10B-40(d). Like the acknowledgment certificate, this attestation will also include the county and state where the notarial act was performed.

There are statutory notary certificates for each type of notarial act for North Carolina notaries to use. However, other certificates are not precluded as long as they include the required elements for the notarial act being performed. G.S. 10B-40(b) through (g).

# Step 7. Sign the Notarial Certificate

Once the notary has completed the attestation of the facts of the notarial act, he or she must sign the certificate with an ink pen in the exact name that is shown on the notary's commission. G.S. 10B-35.

The notary's signature must be signed after the notarial act is performed and must appear on the document in close proximity to the notarial certificate language.

There is a prohibition against a notary signing a notary certificate prior to the performance of a notarial act. In fact, it is an act of official misconduct for a notary to sign blank certificates prior to completing a notarial act. G.S. 10B-35.

## Step 8. Affix the Official Notary Seal

One of the final steps to performing a proper notarial act is for the notary to affix an impression of the official notary seal. The impression of the official notary seal must be placed near the notary's signature and on the same page as the notary certificate wording.

The statute also stipulates that the seal can be affixed only after the notarial act has been performed. G.S. 10B-36(b). Therefore, in no event should a notary ever place his or her official notary seal on a document that has not been completely executed.

## Additional Steps

If a credible witness is used to positively identify the principal signer, an additional oath must be administered to the credible witness by the notary. The notary must ask the credible witness to swear that he or she has no interest in the execution of the document and that the signer has the identity that he or she has claimed to the notary. No additional fee can be charged for administering an oath or affirmation to the credible witness above and beyond the fee charged for the actual notarial act.

# 6
# Notarial Certificates Explained

Completing the Certificate Forms—G.S. 10B-40 . . . . . . . . . . . . 37
Acknowledgment Certificate . . . . . . . . . . . . . . . . . . . . . . . . . . .40
Notarial Certificate for an Oath or Affirmation . . . . . . . . . . . . . . . .43
Administration of Oaths—G.S. 11-2 . . . . . . . . . . . . . . . . . . . . . .46
Affirmation in Lieu of Oath—G.S. 11-4. . . . . . . . . . . . . . . . . . . .47
Oath or Affirmation to Support Constitutions—G.S. 11-7. . . . . . . .47
Verification or Proof Certificate for a Subscribing Witness . . . . .48
Verification or Proof Certificate for a Non-subscribing
Witness. . . . . . . . . . . . . . . . . . . . . . . . . . . . . . . . . . . . . . . . .52
Restrictions on the Use of Proof of Execution Certificates . . . . .54
Notarial Certificates from Other Jurisdictions. . . . . . . . . . . . . . .55
Statutory Certificates for Wills, Powers of Attorney, and
Living Wills . . . . . . . . . . . . . . . . . . . . . . . . . . . . . . . . . . . . . .55
Representative or Fiduciary Capacities . . . . . . . . . . . . . . . . . . .56

## Completing the Certificate Forms—G.S. 10B-40

Completion of the notary certificate is a critical part of the
notarization because the certificate is where the notary
describes exactly what took place during the notarization.
Executed properly, the notary certificate tells the story of who
signed the document, when it was signed, whether the signer
acknowledged his or her signature or took an oath or affirmation indicating that the statements in the document were true,

and where the transaction took place. Proper execution of the notarial certificate will result in a document that can be relied on and trusted by recipients of the document, courts, and any other interested party into perpetuity.

The signed and sealed notary certificate is accepted as prima facie evidence in courts of law the world over. This means that the notary's attestation is accepted as a matter of fact by virtue of the notary's status as a respected public official who is sworn to abide by the notary laws governing the state of North Carolina.

### Important Tips to Remember

- Require satisfactory evidence of identification.
- Require personal appearance.
- Administer an oath or affirmation if the certificate calls for it.
- Ensure that the principal's name and the subscribing witness's name appear in the certificate.

By completing a notary act, the notary attests to the following, even if not specifically stated in the certificate.

- At the time the notarial act was performed and the notarial certificate was signed by the notary public:
  - The notarial act was performed within the geographic limits of the notary public's commission.
  - The principal signer appeared to the notary to be competent and aware of the consequences of having the document notarized. G.S. 10B-40(a2)(2).
  - The principal signer signed the document voluntarily and did not seem to be pressured by anyone else to sign the document. G.S. 10B-40(a2)(2).
  - The notary had a valid commission and was eligible to perform the notarization. G.S. 10B-40(a2)(1).

○ The notarial act was performed in accordance
with the provisions of the notary statutes.
G.S. 10B-40(a2)(2) & (3).

In almost every instance of performing a notarization the
notary will complete a notary certificate, which may be an
acknowledgment, a jurat, or a verification. The only exception
to this is if the notary is administering an oath or affirmation
that is not associated with a document, such as an oath of
office or an oath at a swearing-in ceremony.

When a document is presented to a notary for notarization
and does not include a notary certificate, the notary must ask
the signer what type of notarization is needed.

Notaries are not permitted to determine which type of
notary certificate should be used. To do so would be practicing law, which a notary is not authorized to do and which
could result in disciplinary action being taken against the
notary. In instances where the document does not have a
pre-printed notary certificate, the notary may allow the signer
to choose from all of the certificates in this publication and
select the one that he or she would like the notary to execute.
Another option would be to have the signer consult an attorney or the entity to which the signer is planning to send the
document to determine which notarial act is needed.

After the signer has determined which notarization is needed,
the notary may attach a certificate with the requested notarial
wording to the back of the signature page with a staple or, if
there is room on the document under the principal's signature,
the notary may type or print the statutory wording on the
document itself.

It is important to remember that the notary is not allowed to
select the type of notarization but he or she may provide the
proper notarial certificate once the principal requests a specific notarial act.

Some notary certificates may contain additional information, including the fiduciary or representative capacity in which the principal signed or a statement indicating that he or she was authorized to sign in a specific capacity. Certificates such as these may be used, but the notary is under no obligation to verify the capacity claimed by the signer.

## Acknowledgment Certificate

Although there are statutory acknowledgment certificates for North Carolina notaries' use, certificates from other jurisdictions may be used as long as they include the following components:

- State and county in which the acknowledgment took place, sometimes called the "venue statement."
- Name of the principal who appeared in person before the notary and for whom the notary act is performed.
- An indication that the principal appeared before the notary and signed the record in the notary's presence or that the principal acknowledged to the notary that the principal already signed the record.
- Date when the acknowledgment occurred.
- Signature, seal, or stamp of the notary.
- Notary's expiration date.

If an acknowledgment certificate from another jurisdiction does not include any one of these components, it should not be used and should be replaced with a North Carolina acknowledgment certificate.

When executing an acknowledgment, the signer is acknowledging to the notary that the signature is the principal's and that the principal signed the document willingly. Signing the document in the presence of the notary will accomplish this act since the notary actually witnesses the signer sign. However, if the document is presented with a signature already affixed, the notary must ask the signer if he or she willingly signed the document and the signer must respond in the affirmative. It is perfectly fine for documents requiring an acknowledgment to have been signed prior to being presented to the notary. The notary will simply need to make sure that the signer acknowledges his or her signature. It is not necessary for documents in this situation to be signed again in the notary's presence.

The basic acknowledgment form appears below.

### Basic Acknowledgment Form—G.S. 10B-41

_____ County, North Carolina

I certify that the following person(s) personally appeared before me this day, each acknowledging to me that he or she signed the foregoing document: name(s) of principal(s).

Date: _____  *Official Signature of Notary*

Notary's printed or typed name, Notary Public

My commission expires:

_____

*(Official Seal)*

Besides the notary's signature, the date of notarization, the official seal, and the commission expiration date, the notary's printed name must appear legibly on the certificate. This customarily will be accomplished when the notary affixes the notary seal or stamp as the notary's name will appear legibly within the seal. The appearance of the notary's name in the seal or stamp satisfies the statutory requirement for the notary's printed name.

Below are illustrations of when and how acknowledgment certificates could be completed.

## Acknowledgment Certificate for One Person

*On June 4, 2016, Donald Jones appeared before John Q. Public, a Mecklenburg County notary public, to have his signature notarized. Mr. Jones signed the document in the presence of the notary. The acknowledgment took place in Durham County, NC. Mr. Public's commission expires on May 8, 2021.*

*Donald Jones*

Durham County, North Carolina

I certify that the following person(s) personally appeared before me this day, each acknowledging to me that he or she signed the foregoing document: Donald Jones

Date: June 4, 2016      *John Q. Public*

*John Q. Public*, Notary Public

My commission expires: May 8, 2021

```
┌─────────────────────────────────────┐
│          JOHN Q. PUBLIC             │
│          NOTARY PUBLIC              │
│        Mecklenburg County           │
│         North Carolina              │
│  My Commission Expires May 8, 2021  │
└─────────────────────────────────────┘
```

## Acknowledgment Certificate for Two or More People

*On June 4, 2016, Donald Jones and his wife Mary Jones appeared before a Mecklenburg County notary, John Q. Public, to have their signatures notarized on an already-executed document. (The couple had already signed the document.) The acknowledgment took place in Durham County, NC. Mr. Public's commission expires on May 8, 2021.*

*Donald Jones*
*Mary Jones*

Durham County, North Carolina

    I certify that the following person(s) personally appeared before me this day, each acknowledging to me that he or she signed the foregoing document: Donald Jones and Mary Jones.

Date: June 4, 2016    *John Q. Public*

                   John Q. Public, Notary Public

                   My commission expires: May 8, 2021

```
+--------------------------------------+
|          JOHN Q. PUBLIC              |
|          NOTARY PUBLIC              |
|        Mecklenburg County           |
|          North Carolina             |
|   My Commission Expires May 8, 2021 |
+--------------------------------------+
```

# Notarial Certificate for an Oath or Affirmation

A notarial certificate for an oath or affirmation is commonly called a *jurat*, which is defined as a notary's certificate evidencing the administration of an oath or affirmation.

    Although there is a statutory form for North Carolina notaries, jurat certificates from other jurisdictions may be used if they contain the following components:

- State and county in which the oath or affirmation took place. (Although the statute does not list this as a requirement, this was clearly an oversight and is otherwise included in the samples shown in G.S. 10B-43.)

- Name of the principal who appeared in person before the notary.
- An indication that the principal signed the record and was given an oath or affirmation by the notary.
- Date of the oath or affirmation.
- Signature, seal, or stamp of the notary.
- Notary's expiration date.

There are two primary differences between executing an oath or affirmation and executing an acknowledgment. In the case of an oath or affirmation, the associated document must be signed in the presence of the notary, and the notary administers the oath or affirmation. In the case of an acknowledgment, the acknowledgment may be signed at any time prior to being presented to the notary, in which case the signer indicates to the notary that the signature on the record is the signer's. With an acknowledgment, the signer does not give an oath or affirmation about the truthfulness of the document's contents. An exception to this would be a "hybrid" certificate that refers to acknowledgment of a signature but also indicates that the signer was given an oath or affirmation, in which case the notary must administer an oath or affirmation as a part of the notarial act.

When a notary completes a jurat certificate for an oath or an affirmation, the document must be signed in the presence of the notary. The wording in the jurat certificate demands such because it requires the notary to make a statement that literally states, "The document was signed in my presence." Therefore, any document that has been previously signed and needs to have a jurat certificate will need to be signed again in the presence of the notary when the oath or affirmation is given. The language of the jurat certificate also states that the notary administered an oath or affirmation. As with all notarial acts, the principal must appear in person before the notary at the time of the notarization and present an acceptable form of identification or satisfactory evidence of identity.

An example of an oath or affirmation certificate appears below.

### Oath or Affirmation Certificates—G.S. 10B-43

_____ County, North Carolina

Signed and sworn to before me this day by (name of principal).

Date: _____    _Official Signature of Notary_

_Notary's printed or typed name_, Notary Public

My commission expires: _____

_(Official Seal)_


OR


_____ County, North Carolina

Sworn to and subscribed before me this day by (name of principal).

Date: _____    _Official Signature of Notary_

_Notary's printed or typed name_, Notary Public

My commission expires: _____

_(Official Seal)_


North Carolina's statutory jurat certificate provides space for the name of the principal signer, which should be included each time as a best practice. However, the law allows the principal's name to be omitted as long as the principal whose signature is being notarized is clear from the record. For example, when there is only one principal signing a document, such as on the notary application, it will be clear who signed before the notary and took the oath because there will only be one signature to which the notary's attestation could apply—the applicant's.

In instances where there is one signer and the signature appears just above the jurat wording, it will be clear that the individual to whom the notary's attestation refers could not be anyone other than the principal whose name is subscribed on the document.

The notary must always administer the oath or affirmation before starting the completion of the attestation in the certificate.

## Administration of Oaths—G.S. 11-2

Administering an oath or affirmation when required for the notarial act is critical for the notary because failure to do so is notary misconduct that may result in the revocation of the notary's commission. The notary's role is important in making a record that may be legally necessary to confirm that the principal swore or affirmed that he or she will uphold a standard, abide by some code or set of standards, or swear to the truthfulness of the statements in a document before a public officer.

G.S. 11-2 provides: "Judges and other persons who may be empowered to administer oaths, shall (except in the cases in this Chapter excepted) require the party to be sworn to lay his hand upon the Holy Scriptures, in token of his engagement to speak the truth and in further token that, if he should swerve from the truth, he may be justly deprived of all the blessings of that holy book and made liable to that vengeance which he has imprecated on his own head."

An oath is typically given to a person who swears, invoking the name of a holy deity, with his or her left hand placed on a holy scripture and his or her right hand raised "lifted up toward heaven." (See G.S. 11-3.) The holy scripture need not be the Christian Bible but may be any other sacred book, such as the Torah for people of the Jewish faith, the Koran for Muslims, or the Bhagavad-Gita for Hindus.

The following language is suggested for an oath:

> "Do you *swear* that the facts you have given in this record are the truth, the whole truth, and nothing but the truth, so help you *God?*"

## Affirmation in Lieu of Oath—G.S. 11-4

G.S. 11-4 provides: "When a person to be sworn shall have conscientious scruples against taking an oath in the manner prescribed by G.S. 11-2, 11-3, or 11-7, he shall be permitted to be affirmed. In all cases the words of the affirmation shall be the same as the words of the prescribed oath, except that the word "affirm" shall be substituted for the word "swear" and the words "so help me God" shall be deleted."

The following language is suggested for an affirmation:

> "Do you *affirm*, on your *personal honor*, that the facts you have given in this record are the truth, the whole truth, and nothing but the truth?"

## Oath or Affirmation to Support Constitutions—G.S. 11-7

G.S. 11-7 provides: "Every member of the General Assembly and every person elected or appointed to hold any office of trust or profit in the State shall, before taking office or entering upon the execution of the office, take and subscribe to the following oath:

"I, _____, do solemnly and sincerely swear that I will support the Constitution of the United States; that I will be faithful and bear true allegiance to the State of North Carolina, and to the constitutional powers and authorities which are or may be established for the government thereof; and that I will endeavor to support, maintain and defend the Constitution of said State, not inconsistent with the Constitution of the United States, to the best of my knowledge and ability; so help me God."

North Carolina notaries public also have the authority to administer the oath of office to elected officials. These oaths are given only if a general statute, county resolution, ordinance, or other governing law does not name another authorized person to give the oath of office.

## Verification or Proof Certificate for a Subscribing Witness

A subscribing witness is a person who signs a record for the purpose of being a witness to the principal's execution of the record or to the principal's acknowledgment of his or her execution of the record and is the central character when executing a verification or proof.

This notarial act does not require the principal ever to appear before the notary public—instead, an impartial third party, the subscribing witness, is sent to "prove" that the principal did in fact sign the document. This type of notarial act is not often requested, probably due to the increased risk of fraud.

Because of this disconnect, many entities will not accept this form of notarization. The North Carolina Division of Motor Vehicles (DMV) does not accept a verification or proof on a vehicle title.

Although there are statutory certificates for a verification of a subscribing witness, certificates from other jurisdictions may be used as long as they include the following components:

- State and county in which the verification or proof took place, sometimes called the "venue statement."
- Name of the subscribing witness who appeared in person before the notary and for whom the notary act is performed.
- Name of the principal signer whose signature is to be verified or proven.
- An indication that the notary required personal appearance by the subscribing witness.
- An indication that the subscribing witness took an oath or affirmation before the notary to the fact that the subscribing witness is not a party to or beneficiary of the transaction and signed the original record as a subscribing witness.
- An indication that the subscribing witness took an oath or affirmation before the notary to the fact that either the subscribing witness witnessed the principal signer sign the record or that the principal signer told the subscribing witness that he or she already signed the record.
- Date when the verification or proof occurred.
- Signature, seal, or stamp of the notary.
- Notary's expiration date.

Executing a verification of subscribing witness is unlike any other notarization because the principal signer will not appear before the notary. It is important to understand that although the principal will not appear before the notary, the subscribing witness must do so in the place of the principal.

This type of notarization is also the most complicated in that the notary must administer an oath to the subscribing witness where he or she will either swear or affirm that he or she

- Is not a grantee or beneficiary of the document;
- Signed the document as a subscribing witness;
- Witnessed the principal sign the document; or
- Witnessed the principal acknowledge that he or she willingly signed the document previously.

As is the case with all notarizations, the notary must make sure that the subscribing witness personally appears and presents an acceptable form of identification.

The basic verification or proof certificate appears below.

### Basic Verification or Proof Certificate—G.S. 10B-42

_____ County, North Carolina

I certify that (name of subscribing witness) personally appeared before me this day and certified to me under oath or by affirmation that he or she is not a grantee or beneficiary of the transaction, signed the foregoing document as a subscribing witness, and either (i) witnessed (name of principal) sign the foregoing document or (ii) witnessed (name of principal) acknowledge his or her signature on the already-signed document.

Date: _____  *Official Signature of Notary*

_Notary's printed or typed name_, Notary Public

My commission expires: _____

*(Official Seal)*

Below is an illustration of how a proof certificate could be completed.

## Proof Certificate

*On June 4, 2016, Ruth Middleton appeared before a Mecklenburg County notary, John Q. Public, with a document that had been signed by Donald Jones. Ms. Middleton signed the document as a subscribing witness and affirmed that she witnessed Donald Jones sign the document. She also affirmed that she was not a grantee or beneficiary of the transaction. The proof took place in Wake County, NC. Mr. Public's notary commission expires on May 8, 2021.*

*Donald Jones*

Subscribing Witness: *Ruth Middleton*

Wake County, North Carolina

I certify that Ruth Middleton personally appeared before me this day and certified to me ~~under oath or~~ by affirmation that ~~he or~~ she is not a grantee or beneficiary of the transaction, signed the foregoing document as a subscribing witness, and ~~either (i)~~ witnessed Donald Jones sign the foregoing document. ~~or (ii) witnessed (name of principal) acknowledge his or her signature on the already signed document~~.

Date: June 4, 2016     *John Q. Public*

*John Q. Public*, Notary Public

My commission expires: May 8, 2021

```
JOHN Q. PUBLIC
NOTARY PUBLIC
Mecklenburg County
North Carolina
My Commission Expires May 8, 2021
```

## Verification or Proof Certificate for a Non-subscribing Witness

There is another type of proof that is lawful for a notary to execute. A verification or proof by a non-subscribing witness may be executed if a document that had been executed in the past by either the principal or a subscribing witness is presented to the notary by an impartial third party who swears that the signature of the principal or subscribing witness is genuine.

This is a rare type of notarial act that would only be called for in limited circumstances.

To execute this particular act, an individual must personally appear before the notary with a document that has been previously executed by the principal or a subscribing witness. The notary must positively identify the individual and administer an oath or affirmation where the individual swears or affirms that:

- He or she is not a party to or beneficiary of the transaction.
- He or she recognizes the principal or subscribing witness's signature as genuine.

The non-subscribing witness is not required to sign the document, which differentiates this notarial act from the proof of execution by subscribing witness. A notarial certificate for the verification or proof of the signature of a principal or a subscribing witness by a non-subscribing witness is sufficient if it contains the following:

- State and county in which the verification or proof took place.
- Name of the non-subscribing witness who appeared in person before the notary and for whom the notary act is performed.
- Name of the principal or subscribing witness whose signature on the record is to be verified or proven.

- An indication that the non-subscribing witness took an oath or affirmation to the fact that the non-subscribing witness is not a party to or beneficiary of the transaction.
- An indication that the non-subscribing witness took an oath or affirmation to the fact that the non-subscribing witness recognizes the signature of either the principal signer or the subscribing witness and that the signature is genuine.
- Date when the verification or proof occurred.
- Signature, seal, or stamp of the notary.
- Notary's expiration date.

A notary certificate for a verification of a non-subscribing witness appears below.

### Notary Certificate for a Verification of a Non-subscribing Witness—G.S. 10B-42.1

_____ County, North Carolina

I certify that (name of non-subscribing witness) personally appeared before me this day and certified to me under oath or by affirmation that he or she is not a grantee or beneficiary of the transaction, that (name of non-subscribing witness) recognizes the signature of (name of the principal or the subscribing witness) and that the signature is genuine.

Date: _____      _Official Signature of Notary_

_Notary's printed or typed name_, Notary Public

My commission expires: _____

(Official Seal)

Below is an illustration of how a proof certificate could be completed:

_On June 5, 2016, James Jones appeared before a Mecklenburg County notary, John Q. Public, with a document that had been signed by Michael Davis. Mr. Jones swore that_ the signature of Michael Davis was genuine and that he (Mr. Jones) was not a grantee or beneficiary of the transaction. The proof took place in Wake County, NC. Mr. Public's notary commission expires on May 8, 2021.

*Michael Davis*

## Proof Certificate by Non-subscribing Witness

Wake County, North Carolina

I certify that James Jones personally appeared before me this day and certified to me under oath ~~or by affirmation~~ that he ~~or she~~ is not a grantee or beneficiary of the transaction, that James Jones recognizes the signature of Michael Davis, and that the signature is genuine.

Date: June 5, 2016      *John Q. Public*

*John Q. Public*, Notary Public

My commission expires: May 8, 2021

# Restrictions on the Use of Proof of Execution Certificates

A proof of execution will normally be used in place of an acknowledgment when the principal is not able to appear before the notary personally. It may also be used to prove the signature of a subscribing witness.

A proof may never be used in place of a document requiring an oath or affirmation because no one may take an oath on behalf of another individual.

Proofs also are not allowed on Division of Motor Vehicle titles or any other DMV documents.

## Notarial Certificates from Other Jurisdictions

Any notarial certificate made in another jurisdiction shall be sufficient in this state if it is made in accordance with federal law or the laws of the jurisdiction where the notarial certificate is made. G.S. 10B-40(e). There can be a difference between a sufficient notarial certificate and what is required on a form for recording in a public office. For example, instruments may need to have certain components in the notarial certificate to be acceptable to the Department of Motor Vehicles or the registers of deeds offices regardless of whether those components are required for the notarial certificate to be legally valid. The notary does not give advice about such matters. The notary complies with the notary laws.

On records to be filed, registered, recorded, or delivered in another state or jurisdiction of the United States, a North Carolina notary public may complete any notarial certificate that may be required in that other state or jurisdiction. This, however, does not authorize North Carolina notaries to perform notarial acts that are not authorized by North Carolina notary law. For example, if the out-of-state certificate requires the notary to certify a copy of a document, the notary could not complete the certificate because copy certification is not a power authorized by North Carolina notary law.

## Statutory Certificates for Wills, Powers of Attorney, and Living Wills

The North Carolina General Statutes that govern wills, powers of attorney, and living wills provide specific notarial certificates that must be used. These certificates should not be replaced with the standard notary certificates in G.S. Chapter 10B.

There are also a wide variety of notary certificates found in G.S. Chapter 47 for documents ranging from corporate conveyances to affidavits. These certificates may be replaced by appropriate certificates in G.S. Chapter 10B without consequence.

## Representative or Fiduciary Capacities

When performing any notarial act, it is the notary's responsibility to identify the signer as an individual person; for example, Mary Smith or Jane Collins. In some instances, a person may sign the record in a representative or fiduciary capacity, such as a president or a guardian.

If an individual signs a record and claims to be acting in a representative or fiduciary capacity, the signer is representing to the notary that he or she is signing the record on behalf of the person or entity represented and that he or she has the authority to do so.

A notary public is under no duty to verify whether the individual acted in a representative or fiduciary capacity or, if so, whether the individual was duly authorized to do so. A notarial certificate may include any of the following:

- A statement that an individual signed a record in a particular representative or fiduciary capacity.
- A statement that the individual who signed the record in a representative or fiduciary capacity had due authority to do so.
- A statement identifying the represented person or entity or the fiduciary capacity.

# 7
# Special Circumstances

Unique Notarial Acts. . . . . . . . . . . . . . . . . . . . . . . . . . . . . . . .57
   Signature by Mark—G.S. 10B-20(d) . . . . . . . . . . . . . . . . . . . . . . .58
   Principal Is Physically Disabled—G.S. 10B-20(e) . . . . . . . . . . . . . . .58
   Inventory of Abandoned Safe Deposit Box—G.S. 53C-6-13(a). . . . . .59
   Court Reporter's Certification—G.S. 1A-1, Rules of Civil
     Procedure—Rule 30 . . . . . . . . . . . . . . . . . . . . . . . . . . . . . .60

Signing Agents, Settlement Agents, Closing Agents, and
  Mobile Notaries. . . . . . . . . . . . . . . . . . . . . . . . . . . . . . . . . . .62

Reasons to Refuse to Notarize a Document. . . . . . . . . . . . . . . .63
   Lack of a Notary Certificate . . . . . . . . . . . . . . . . . . . . . . . . . . . .65
   Foreign Language Certificates. . . . . . . . . . . . . . . . . . . . . . . . . . .65
   False or Fraudulent Certificates . . . . . . . . . . . . . . . . . . . . . . . . .66

Voter Absentee Application. . . . . . . . . . . . . . . . . . . . . . . . . . . .66

Division of Motor Vehicles Documentation . . . . . . . . . . . . . . . .68

## Unique Notarial Acts

There are circumstances when a notary is called upon to perform unique notarial acts that may provide a valued service
to persons with special needs or acts that are set out in other
sections of the North Carolina General Statutes. For example,
a principal may be incapacitated or simply unable to execute
a document by signing a traditional signature, the notary may
be asked to certify the contents of an abandoned safe deposit
box in a bank, or a court reporter notary may be required to

certify the accuracy of a transcript in a deposition or court proceeding. How the notary is to proceed in each of these unique circumstances is described below.

## Signature by Mark—G.S. 10B-20(d)

If a principal is unable to sign his or her own name, the principal may place a mark in lieu of a traditional signature on the document requiring the notarization. The principal's mark has the same legal validity as a traditional signature and may be made by pen, facsimile stamp, thumbprint, or other means. The mark must be made in the presence of the notary.

Immediately beneath the mark the notary must write the following statement:

> Mark affixed by (name of signer by mark) in presence of undersigned notary.

This procedure must be used in any circumstance where the signer is not able to sign a traditional signature, including when a signer uses a facsimile stamp as his or her signature.

The type of notarial act required will not be impacted by the method used to affix the signature on the document.

## Principal Is Physically Disabled—G.S. 10B-20(e)

If a principal is physically unable to sign, cannot move his or her arms, and cannot hold a pen in his or her mouth or with any other appendage to make a mark, the disabled person may designate another person to sign for him or her.

The designee cannot be a signer or party to the document and must be a disinterested person who has no financial or beneficial interest in the transaction. To execute this type of notarization, the disabled principal signer must direct the designee to sign the document in the principal's name while in the presence of the notary and two impartial witnesses. The two witnesses must then sign their respective names near the principal's signature on the document as witnesses.

The notary must then write the following statement below the principal's signature:

Signature affixed by (designee) in the presence of (names and address of principal and witnesses).

The notary then notarizes the signature through an acknowledgment, oath or affirmation, jurat, or verification.

In this unique situation, five people will be involved in this notarization—the disabled principal, the principle's designee, witness number one, witness number two, and the notary.

## Inventory of Abandoned Safe Deposit Box—G.S. 53C-6-13(a)

Notaries are also authorized to inventory abandoned safe deposit boxes. When payment for a safe deposit box is overdue, the bank usually sends a notice by registered mail or certified mail, return receipt requested, to the last known address of the lessee stating that the safe deposit box will be opened and its contents stored at the expense of the lessee unless payment of the rental is made within 30 days.

If the rental is not paid within 30 days from the mailing of the notice, the box may be opened in the presence of an officer of the bank and a notary public who is not a director, officer, employee, or stockholder of the bank. While in the presence of a bank official, the notary public opens and empties the contents of the safe deposit box. The notary inventories the items found in the box by writing a description of each item on a special package provided by the bank. The notary executes a certificate, writing on it the name of the lessee, the date the box was opened, and a list of its contents, and puts it in the package. After all the items are inventoried, the notary places each item into the package, seals it in the presence of the bank official, and writes on the outside the name of the lessee and the date of the opening. A copy of the certificate will be sent by the bank by registered mail or certified mail, return receipt requested, to the last known address of the lessee. The package will then be placed in the general vaults of the bank.

Figure 1 presents a sample of one of the simpler certificates in use today. Other banks have longer, more involved forms.

## Court Reporter's Certification—G.S. 1A-1, Rules of Civil Procedure—Rule 30

Rule 30(f) of the Rules of Civil Procedure requires the following:

> The person administering the oath shall certify that the deponent was duly sworn by him and that the deposition is a true record of the testimony given by the deponent. This certificate shall be in writing and accompany the sound-and-visual or sound recording or transcript of the deposition. . . .

In the past, court reporters placed their notary seal on the certificate page in deposition transcripts. The Administrative Office of the Courts, in conjunction with the Secretary of State's office, determined that certificate pages *should not contain a notary seal, as court reporters should not appear to be notarizing their own signatures.*

A court reporter can comply with Rule 30 of the Rules of Civil Procedure without placing a notary seal on the certificate. The method that the court reporter must follow is to place his or her notary number under his or her name on the certificate page without affixing the notary seal. The notary's unique commissioning number should only be used for official actions within the court system as it is a unique number and could be used unlawfully to glean personal information about the notary.

# Figure 1. Certificate of Inventory of Safe Deposit Box

## Certificate of Inventory of a Safe Deposit Box

| Financial Center Name/Address | | | | Financial Center Number |
|---|---|---|---|---|

| Safe Deposit Box Number | Annual Rent Amount | Drilling Fee Amount | Date Box Drilled | Date Box Opened |
|---|---|---|---|---|

| Lessee Name | Customer SSN | Address | |
|---|---|---|---|
| Lessee Name | Customer SSN | Address | |

Reason for drilling/opening the safe deposit box when the Lessee is **NOT** present:

☐ Nonpayment of rent (all states except FL/NJ/PA/TN)      ☐ Lost keys - Lessee states box is empty

☐ Box closed - Lessee requests by mail to terminate the lease      ☐ Other (describe): _____

On the above date, in accordance with state law, the rules and regulations of _____ Bank and the Agreement entered into with the Lessee, this Bank, in the presence of the undersigned, caused said safe deposit box to be drilled/opened and the contents thereof removed and inventoried as follows:

**Description and Quantity of Each Item** (Use generic terms such as **2 gold-colored rings, 1 clear stone ring**).

☐ **Check Here if BOX is EMPTY**

_____

The contents listed above have been sealed in Deposit Bag Number _____, labeled with the Lessee's name and box number. These contents have been stored in dual control vault number _____,

located at _____ .

Signed: _____          Signed: _____
        Bank Representative                        Lock Technician's Name (if box is drilled)

Title: _____          Company: _____

Signed: _____
        Notary Public                     (Seal)

My Commission Expires: _____

### Complete if customer claims contents

I have received sealed Deposit Bag Number _____

| | Customer Signature | Date |
|---|---|---|

| Bank Representative Releasing Contents | Date | Customer Signature | Date |
|---|---|---|---|

562448 (Rev 04) Page 1 of 1      Original - Attach to Signature Card      Copy - Mail to Lessee      Copy - Attach to contents

## Signing Agents, Settlement Agents, Closing Agents, and Mobile Notaries

Signing agents are not recognized in North Carolina notary law, and the Secretary of State does not seek to regulate such practices. Because notaries are hired as signing agents by virtue of the fact that they have a valid notary commission and an important function of a signing agent is to notarize specific documents, the Department emphasizes that all notaries, including any who work as signing agents, must adhere to all statutory guidelines for notaries. The guidelines include the following:

- Notaries *must in no way engage in the unauthorized practice of law* when serving in this capacity.
- Notaries are *not authorized to charge (the borrowers/ buyers/grantors) a higher fee than the statutory limit of $5.00 per signature* when performing these or any other notarizations.
- Notaries are *not authorized to charge travel or mileage expenses* to their clients.
- Notaries must always follow the North Carolina General Statutes and avoid the unauthorized practice of law, codified at G.S. 84-2.1.

The State Bar has opined in its Authorized Practice Advisory Opinion 2002-1 (revised January 26, 2012) On the Role of Laypersons in the Consummation of Residential Real Estate Transactions that a non-lawyer may (1) present and identify the documents necessary to complete a North Carolina residential real estate closing, direct the parties where to sign the documents, and ensure that the parties have properly executed the documents; and (2) receive and disburse the closing funds.

The opinion also made clear that these are ministerial functions and that non-lawyers may not perform any activities that would constitute the practice of law, which would include giving advice, preparing documents, or solving disputes, among many other things.

*Signing agent* is broadly defined as a person holding a notary commission who is specifically trained to facilitate the mortgage closing process.

A signing agent collects and notarizes signatures and delivers settlement checks for mortgage lenders, title firms, and escrow companies without the presence of a licensed attorney. Signing agents, also called *closing agents* or *settlement agents*, work with the mortgage companies or attorneys to "close" loans by notarizing the borrowers'/buyers'/grantors' signatures on loan documents. Notaries who are hired by a mortgage company, title firm, or escrow company must be certain not to overstep statutory limitations in performing notarizations in these settings.

If a notary public is found to be in violation of any notary laws, the notary's commission may be revoked. The notary's case is also referred to the appropriate agency for further sanctions (for example, the North Carolina State Bar if the notary has engaged in the unauthorized practice of law).

A *mobile notary* is simply a notary public who travels to people's homes or businesses to notarize signatures. All of the notary laws and all of the above limitations apply to notaries engaging in this activity.

## Reasons to Refuse to Notarize a Document

There are various reasons for a notary to refuse to notarize a document. Three of the most important reasons for not performing a notarial act are (1) the signer does not *appear in person* before the notary at the time of the notarization, (2) the principal does not possess *satisfactory evidence* of identification, or (3) the notary suspects that the document is fraudulent or will be used for fraudulent purposes.

Additional reasons for refusing to notarize a document include, but are not limited to, the following:

- The notary is a signer of, or an interested party to, or a beneficiary, or a grantor, or otherwise named in some other capacity in the document. There are some exceptions to this rule, including when the notary

    - is also serving as the *trustee in a deed of trust,*
    - is the *drafter* of the record,
    - is the person *to whom the document will be sent* after recording, or
    - is the *attorney of record* to a party of the document as long as the attorney who is acting as the notary is not also a party to the record *individually* or in some other representative or fiduciary capacity.

G.S. 10B-20(c)(5).

The notary will receive an additional consideration *over and beyond the fees* that are authorized by G.S. 10B-31, other than fees, cash, interest, property, and commissions, etc., paid for services rendered by

- an *attorney* licensed to practice law in North Carolina,
- a *real estate broker or salesperson* licensed to do business in North Carolina,
- a *motor vehicle dealer,* or
- a *banker.*

G.S. 10B-20(c)(6).

However, a notary who is an employee of a party shall not be disqualified solely because of the notary's employment by a party to the record or solely because the notary owns stock in a party to the record. G.S. 10B-20(c)(5).

## Lack of a Notary Certificate

If the document presented for notarization does not have a notary certificate, the notary cannot perform a notarization. In such instances, the signer will have to tell the notary what type of notarization is required. Typically the signer will not know what to request and will look to the notary for guidance. It is imperative that the notary *not* suggest or recommend that a specific notarial act be performed as this would constitute the unauthorized practice of law. The notary may provide this publication and allow the signer to choose from the certificates listed, or the notary may direct the signer to the Department's website and have the signer select a certificate of his or her choosing. The signer may also consult an attorney or the drafter of the document for assistance in determining which certificate to choose. Notaries are ministerial officials and as such are prohibited from drafting documents, making recommendations, or giving advice. Once the principal decides on a type of notarial certificate, the notary may attach the certificate to the back of the signature page and execute the notarization.

## Foreign Language Certificates

Notaries are prohibited from completing notarial certificates written in a foreign language. If presented with a non–English language certificate, the notary must refuse to notarize the document.

Documents written in a foreign language may be notarized as long as the notarial certificate is in the English language. Therefore, if the signer selects an English language certificate, the notary will be able to perform the notarization on a document written in a foreign language. G.S. 10B-22(b).

## False or Fraudulent Certificates

If the notarial certificate contains information that the notary believes to be false, the notary must refuse to notarize the document. G.S. 10B-22(a). This would include any information contained in the certificate, such as the date, the name of the signer appearing before the notary, a representative capacity known to be untrue, or other false statements.

Because the notary has complete authority over the completion of the notary certificate (since it is his or her attestation), the notary has the liberty to make corrections to any incorrect statements in the notary certificate. Common mistakes include dates that were already filled in or instances where the name of the husband and wife were inserted in the certificate but the individuals appear before the notary at different times. In the latter case, the notary would simply correct the date or line through the absent spouse's name on the certificate.

## Voter Absentee Application

North Carolina's absentee voter application and certificate is required to be witnessed either by two witnesses *or* by one notary. If witnessed by one notary, the notary will need to complete the "Alternative Notary-Witness Certification" section of the form. Figure 2 presents an example of the absentee application and certificate.

The absentee voter application and certificate represents a new notarial act distinctly different from an acknowledgment, oath, or verification. In executing this act, the notary must take the following steps:

1. Require personal appearance of the voter.
2. Positively identify the voter.
3. Witness the voter mark his or her ballot.

# Figure 2. Absentee Application and Certificate

**[COUNTY] COUNTY**
**ABSENTEE APPLICATION AND CERTIFICATE**

FRAUDULENTLY OR FALSELY COMPLETING THIS FORM IS
A CLASS I FELONY UNDER CHAPTER 163 OF THE NC GENERAL STATUTES.

---

AFFIX VOTER INFORMATION

LABEL HERE

**VOTER'S CERTIFICATION**

I do hereby certify that I am a duly qualified voter, registered as an affiliate of the political party indicated on this application, that all information represented is correct, and that I am entitled to vote in this election. If I am an Unaffiliated voter voting in a primary election, I am voting in the Party Primary indicated: (DEM) (REP) or (LIB). If the party indicated is (UNA), I am voting a nonpartisan ballot.

I certify that I am making application for an absentee ballot, and that I marked the ballot enclosed herein (or it was marked for me in my presence and according to my instructions) in the presence of two witnesses who are at least 18 years of age and who are not disqualified by law to witness the casting of my absentee ballot.

AFFIX ABSENTEE

BARCODE LABEL

HERE

X _____
Signature of Voter (Required)          Date

_____
Name correction (if applicable)

**CERTIFICATION OF PERSON ASSISTING VOTER (if applicable)**

BOARD APPROVAL:

I certify that I assisted the voter in marking his or her ballot according to his or her instruction and/or I assisted the voter in signing this certificate because the voter is unable to complete and/or sign this certification

_____
Date

Name of Person Assisting Voter (if applicable)     Address of Person Assisting Voter

X _____
Signature of Person Assisting Voter          Date

**WITNESSES' CERTIFICATION**
(Two witnesses are required unless witnessed by a notary public)

I certify that I am at least 18 years of age and am not disqualified by G.S. 163-226.3(a)(4) or G.S. 163-237(b1) to assist this voter in marking or witnessing the casting of his/her absentee ballot, and in my presence, the voter marked the enclosed ballot, or caused it to be marked in his/her presence according to his/her instruction, and signed this absentee application and certificate.

X _____
Witness #1 Signature (Required)

_____
Witness #1 Street Address (Required)

_____
Witness #1 City, State, Zip (Required)

X _____
Witness #2 Signature (Required)

_____
Witness #2 Street Address (Required)

_____
Witness #2 City, State, Zip (Required)

**ALTERNATIVE NOTARY-WITNESS CERTIFICATION**
(Use this section only if witnessing this certificate and application as a notary public.)

State of _____ County of _____

I certify that I am at least 18 years of age and am not disqualified by G.S. 163-226.3(a)(4) or G.S. 163-237(b1) to assist this voter in marking or witnessing the casting of his/her absentee ballot. On the _____ day of _____, 20____, the voter

_____
Print Voter's Name

personally appeared before me, was positively identified, and in my presence, marked the enclosed ballot, or caused it to be marked in his or her presence according to his or her instruction, and signed this absentee application and certificate.

X _____
Signature of Notary Public

_____
My Commission Expires

**SECOND PRIMARY OR RUNOFF REQUEST**

In the event that a Second Primary (or Runoff Election) is called, with my signature below, I request that an absentee application and ballot be issued to me and mailed to me at the address given below.

X _____
Signature of Voter (if applicable)

_____
Address Where Application and Ballot Should be Mailed

**ANNUAL REQUEST FOR SICKNESS/PHYSICAL DISABILITY**

Due to continued or expected illness or disability, I request that this application be a request for absentee ballots for any other elections to be held this calendar year in which I am eligible to participate.

X _____
Signature of Voter (if applicable)

_____
Address Where Application and Ballot Should be Mailed

NCSBOE v2013.11

4. Witness the voter seal his or her ballot in the provided envelope.
5. Witness the voter sign the voter's certification.
6. Complete the notary witness certification section of the application including the venue and the certificate wording.
7. Sign the certificate and affix the official notary seal directly onto the sealed envelope where the "Alternative Notary-Witness Certification" appears.

G.S. 163-231(a).

The notary-witness may also be required to assist the voter in marking the ballot if the voter is not physically able to do so on his or her own. In such a case, the notary would need to complete the "Certification of Assisting Voter" section in addition to the notary witness certification described above.

The absentee voter application and certificate comes with a detailed instruction sheet for the voter and provides minimal instructions for the notary.

Notaries *are not allowed to charge for this notarial act.* G.S. 10B-30(d).

## Division of Motor Vehicles Documentation

All applications for a North Carolina title and all assignments of North Carolina titles must be personally acknowledged before a notary public or before a person having authority to administer oaths. Several general principles apply to motor vehicle certifications, no matter which of the Division of Motor Vehicles (DMV) forms are being used.

Six items constitute a proper assignment of a title document:

• Buyer's name and address
• Date of delivery of vehicle to buyer

- Odometer reading and certification (10 years old or newer)
- Seller's signature in Section A
- Notarization
- Damage disclosure statement

The notary must be certain that all blanks for the buyer's name and address, the seller's name, the odometer reading, and the damage disclosure statement are filled in before taking the acknowledgment.

DMV requires that signatures on title documents be acknowledged. A proof of execution is invalid; personal appearance is required.

DMV forms no longer require the administration of an oath before acknowledging signatures, but if the form contains a jurat "sworn to and subscribed before me," the notary must administer an oath to the person signing.

The seller should sign his or her name exactly as it is printed on the face of the title.

The notary should require full printed names and signatures; this means that a person's middle name should be included. Titles such as "Mr.," "Mrs.," "Ms.," "Dr.," etc., should not be used.

The notary should be especially careful not to make spelling or other errors. If an error is made in the first or middle name because of a misspelling or a nickname, the notary should not erase it or white it out; instead, he or she should draw one line through the error and then correct it above or to the side of the error. If the error is in the last name, an affidavit is required.

Any alteration in the last name makes the assignment void. Affidavits from the seller, buyer, and lien holder are required. A new assignment without alterations is required.

# 8
# Notary Violations

Notary Public Act Enforcement—G.S. 10B-60. . . . . . . . . . . . . . 71
  Professional Unfitness . . . . . . . . . . . . . . . . . . . . . . . . . . . . . . 72
  Misdemeanors and Felonies. . . . . . . . . . . . . . . . . . . . . . . . . 73
Illegal Practices in the Mortgage Industry. . . . . . . . . . . . . . . . 74
Illegal Actions Involving "Sovereign Citizens". . . . . . . . . . . . . 75
The Right to Refuse Service. . . . . . . . . . . . . . . . . . . . . . . . . . . 77
The Most Common Notary Violations. . . . . . . . . . . . . . . . . . . 78
The Top 10 Notary Violations . . . . . . . . . . . . . . . . . . . . . . . . . 78
How to File a Complaint. . . . . . . . . . . . . . . . . . . . . . . . . . . . . . 79
Limitations on the Notary's Authority . . . . . . . . . . . . . . . . . . 82
Advertising Notary Public Services in a Language Other
  Than English . . . . . . . . . . . . . . . . . . . . . . . . . . . . . . . . . . . . 82
Posting Fees in English . . . . . . . . . . . . . . . . . . . . . . . . . . . . . . 82
Certifying a True Copy or Notarizing or Authenticating a
  Photograph . . . . . . . . . . . . . . . . . . . . . . . . . . . . . . . . . . . . . 83
Using the Notary's Official Seal as an Endorsement for
  Anything . . . . . . . . . . . . . . . . . . . . . . . . . . . . . . . . . . . . . . . . 83

## Notary Public Act Enforcement—G.S. 10B-60

Notaries have an obligation to follow the notary laws in the execution of their duties. In fact, when notaries take the oath of office they swear or affirm that they will execute the duties of the office of notary public according to the best of their skills and abilities, according to the law. The North Carolina Secretary of State has the authority and obligation to enforce the notary laws and may deny, suspend, or revoke a notary's commission for violating the notary law.

The Secretary of State may also administer discipline through written warnings, remanding notaries to attend educational courses, and restricting an individual's ability to obtain a notary commission. Disciplinary action may be taken for a variety of activities, ranging from actions deemed to be against the public's best interest to criminal activities that could result in imprisonment.

The Department of the Secretary of State has a notary enforcement division that includes sworn law enforcement agents with statewide jurisdiction and all of the powers and authority of law enforcement officers to investigate criminal activity and apprehend those suspected of violating the law. G.S. 10B-60(g).

Once the Secretary of State has launched an investigation into possible notary misconduct, the sudden resignation of the notary will not have any bearing on the Department's investigation. G.S. 10B-60(h).

There are specific violations in the notary law that may result in misdemeanors, felonies, or a showing of professional unfitness under G.S. 84-28(d).

## Professional Unfitness

The Secretary of State is obligated to notify and provide to the North Carolina State Bar copies of any court order or final decision finding a violation of the notary act by a notary who is also an attorney-at-law licensed under G.S. Chapter 84.

Any referral by the Secretary of State to the State Bar will be considered a showing of professional unfitness under G.S. 84-28(d), and the State Bar shall administer discipline accordingly.

## Misdemeanors and Felonies

Class 1 misdemeanors may result from someone impersonating a notary; performing a notarial act with an expired,
suspended, or revoked commission; or performing a
notarization before being properly sworn in as a notary.
G.S. 10B-60(b).

Other violations that may result in Class 1 misdemeanors
are performing any notarial act without requiring personal
appearance and performing any notarial act without requiring
positive identification of the principal signer. G.S. 10B-60(c).

A Class I felony would typically result from a notary performing any notarial act with the knowledge that it is false or
fraudulent. Any notary who performs a notarial act without
requiring personal appearance and is found to have had the
intent to commit fraud could also be found guilty of a Class I
felony. G.S. 10B-60(d).

It is a Class I felony for any person to perform notarial acts
in this state knowing that he or she does not have a notary
commission. G.S. 10B-60(e). It is also a Class I felony for any
person to obtain, use, conceal, deface, or destroy the seal or
records of a notary. G.S. 10B-60(f).

Any person who wrongfully obtains, conceals, damages,
or destroys the certificate, disk, coding, card, program, software, file, or hardware enabling an electronic notary to affix
an official electronic signature is guilty of a Class I felony.
G.S. 10B-146.

Any person who knowingly creates, manufactures, or distrib-
utes software for the purpose of allowing a person to act as an
electronic notary without being commissioned and registered
in accordance with the Notary Act shall be guilty of a Class G
felony. G.S. 10B-146.

Any person who knowingly solicits, coerces, or in any material way influences a notary to commit official misconduct is
guilty as an aider and abettor and is subject to the same level
of punishment as the notary. G.S. 10B-60(j).

There are other violations that may not rise to the status of a misdemeanor or felony but are harmful to the public and may be punishable by suspension or revocation of a notary's commission. Some of these acts involve failure to meet the statutory requirements for notarization, including the following:

1. Incomplete attestation
2. Improper acknowledgment language
3. Incorrect signature
4. Incorrect expiration date
5. Failure to administer an oath or affirmation
6. Failure to verify identification
7. Failure to require personal appearance
8. Notarization of a document in which the notary is a named, interested, or signed party
9. Notarization of a "non-signature" or a copy of a signature
10. Charging a fee in excess of that which is set by law, including fees for mileage or travel
11. Acting as a notary when not commissioned
12. Unauthorized use of a seal

18 NCAC 07B .0904

## Illegal Practices in the Mortgage Industry

The mortgage industry has been ravaged in recent years as a result of policies that required notaries to notarize documents for individuals who never actually appeared before the notary. This illegal process became widely referred to as "robo-signing." Particularly troublesome is a practice by which notaries completed attestations certifying that a specific person personally appeared before them and willingly signed a document or took an oath swearing that the information in the document was true when neither actually occurred. This practice opens the notary up to being charged with several felonies—including failure to require satisfactory evidence of identity and failure to require personal appearance, both with the intent to commit fraud.

## Illegal Actions Involving "Sovereign Citizens"

Bogus Uniform Commercial Code (UCC) filings have become more common in recent years due to the increasing numbers of people who identify with an anti-government belief system called the "sovereign citizen movement," a loose network of individuals living across the United States who believe that the government is illegitimate. The Federal Bureau of Investigation (FBI) has designated sovereign citizens a domestic terrorist movement and a growing threat to law enforcement. Many of these individuals use paper-based tactics to strike back at government interference in their lives. Numerous websites sell how-to kits or offer to train subscribers on how to perpetrate filing schemes in exchange for large fees.

Most of these filings utilize telltale buzzwords and share common indicators, including the following:

- References to the Bible, the Constitution, U.S. Supreme Court decisions, or foreign treaties
- Names written in all capital letters or interspersed with colons
- Signatures followed by the words "under duress," "Sovereign Living Soul," or a copyright symbol
- Personal seals, stamps, or thumbprints in red ink
- The words "accepted for value"
- Copies of personal documents, such as birth certificates or Social Security cards

Sometimes called "freemen" and "strawmen," these so-called sovereign citizens sometimes use fake quit-claim deeds. A March 10, 2011, CNN article entitled "'Sovereign Citizens'

Fraudulently Taking over Foreclosed Homes" reported that "[t]he FBI said sovereign citizens are responsible for many crimes, including impersonating police officers, threatening judges and using fake currency and documents."

In many cases notaries do not have the authority to perform the acts that are often required with sovereign citizen documents, resulting in notaries being sanctioned for exceeding their powers and limitations. Some of the more common documents that are presented by sovereign citizens are

- Act of State
- Presentment under Notary Seal
- Notary's Certificate of Service
- Verification of Mailings
- Public Notice, Declarations, and Lawful Protest
- Conveyance Bond
- Affidavit of Notary Presentment—Certificate of Mailing
- Affidavit of Political Status
- Power of Attorney
- Hold Harmless and Indemnity Agreement
- Private Registered Bond for Set-Off
- Verified Affidavit of Facts
- Affidavit of Individual Surety

In addition to the types of documents sovereign citizens are likely to present, the language used in the documents can also be an indicator that a notary is dealing with a sovereign citizen. Some of the common phrases that appear in their documents in North Carolina are

- ...I AM; the Divine Spirit having a human experience
- a natural born Divine creation, and a Private, Sentient
- certify the Sentient Signature in the Archetype Document enclosed to be a true ...
- ...the undersigned, a Wazi (Notary Public) for the Moorish national Republic Federal Government ...

- ...All Moorish American Nationals Aboriginal Indigenous Divine Beings manifested in human flesh ...
- ...We, the Divine Spirit, expressed in trust in living flesh, having returned from being lost in the sea of illusion ...
- ...I AM one with the light, one with Creator, the alpha and the omega, without beginning nor end, without time ...

## The Right to Refuse Service

Notaries are appointed to serve the public and should honor all lawful and reasonable requests for notarial services. However, the law prohibits a notary from completing a notarial certificate if he or she believes it contains false information. G.S. 10B-22(a).

It is also unlawful for a notary to notarize a document knowing that it contains false, dishonest, or fraudulent information. Examples of such dishonest acts include

- Notarizing a blank DMV vehicle title document
- Embezzlement
- Forgery
- Fraud
- Identity theft
- Impersonation of a law enforcement officer
- Receiving stolen goods or property
- Theft

Therefore, notaries have a legal obligation to refuse to notarize if they have reason to believe that the document is false, fraudulent, or will be used for dishonest intent. 18 NCAC 07B .0903.

When faced with individuals or documents that purport to be from the sovereign citizen movement, notaries should take care to ensure that they do not perform acts not authorized by statute. Notaries should also take their personal safety into account as some elements in the sovereign citizen movement have been known to commit violent acts against those who oppose them.

## The Most Common Notary Violations

The notary law has been crafted to protect the public's interest, and in order for it to have its intended impact notaries must follow the law without exception. Indeed, most notaries find themselves being disciplined by the Department because they violated the law trying to "help" someone in a difficult position.

Often, a notary notarizes for someone who does not personally appear because a signer tells the notary a sad story about a spouse not being able to be present and only having limited time to get the document notarized before being doomed to some incredible unfortunate fate. What generally happens in such a case is that the signature is forged, the unsuspecting spouse loses his or her interest in something of value, and the notary is sanctioned for trying to help. The best thing notaries can do in every situation is to follow the letter of the law. By doing so, they protect our citizens and the integrity of the notary process.

## The Top 10 Notary Violations

Below are the top 10 notary complaints received by the Department:

1. Notarizing without requiring personal appearance
2. Exceeding powers and limitations
3. Executing incomplete acknowledgments

4. Notarizing forged signatures
5. Executing improper acknowledgments
6. Certifying true copies
7. Notarizing non-signatures
8. Notarizing while not holding a valid notary commission
9. Notarizing the notary's own signature
10. Failing to include the correct notary expiration date on the certificate

## How to File a Complaint

Complaints against North Carolina notaries public may be filed by completing a Complaint Form, which can be found on the Department's website at **www.sosnc.gov**.

From the **Notary Public Home Page**

1. Select "Notary Complaints" from the menu.
2. From the "Tip and Complaint Forms" menu click on Notary Complaint Form under the "Notary Enforcement" heading.
3. Fill out the form by providing detailed information. Be specific and compose clear, concise answers.

Furnish copies of any documents or other materials relating to the complaint. Submit the Complaint Form and documentation by mail, fax to 919.807.2130, or email to **Notary@sosnc.gov**.

In addition to the Notary Complaint form, there is a specific complaint form for notary complaints related to mortgage fraud, which can be obtained from the Department.

The Department will investigate all viable complaints of notary misconduct.

## Notary Dos and Don'ts
### Do:

- Sign the certificate in exactly the name that appears on your commission and seal.
- Ensure personal appearance of the signer when performing a notarial act.
- Place your seal image near your signature.
- Insist on a current form of acceptable identification if you do not personally know the document signer.
- Keep track of your commission expiration date and make sure it is included on every certificate you complete.
- Keep sole control of your notary seal.
- Ensure that you make a legible impression of your embossed seal or stamp each time you affix it to a notary certificate.
- Ensure that the information in your certificate matches the facts of the notarial act.
- Ensure that your printed or typed name appears in the certificate.
- Ensure that the certificate is appropriate and complete.
- Cross out blank spaces in certificates except when a blank is specifically allowed by law.
- When required to administer an oath or an affirmation, be sure to do so.
- Report any change of status including a name, address, email address, phone number, work address, criminal conviction, or any other change of status to the Secretary of State within 45 days of the change.
- Include the name of the person you are notarizing for in the notary certificate.
- Require the seller's presence when notarizing a DMV "First Re-assignment by Owner."

**Don't:**

- Sign a different name than the name that appears on your commission and notary seal.
- Take someone's acknowledgment over the telephone or by mail, email, conference call, webinar, etc.
- Place your seal image on a different page than your signature.
- Rely on the identification of the signer by a credible witness not personally known to you.
- Perform a notary act after your commission expires.
- Loan or give your seal to anyone else.
- Use a seal or stamp that creates an image too light to be seen when the document is copied.
- Use a pre-printed certificate if it does not accurately reflect the notarization you have performed (wrong names, wrong dates, etc.)
- Omit your typed or printed name in the certificate.
- Complete a certificate that is not in the English language.
- Select the type of notarial act to perform when the document is presented without any notary language.
- Complete a certificate involving an oath or affirmation without administering one.
- Sign with a name that does not match your seal.
- Sign and seal a document without a complete notarial certificate.
- Notarize your own signature.
- Notarize a DMV "First Re-assignment by Owner" certificate without the buyer's name and address in the certificate.
- Charge for mileage in addition to the statutory fee for performing notarizations.
- Charge more than the statutory fee for performing any notarization.

## Limitations on the Notary's Authority

Notaries *cannot* perform the following acts:

1. Assist persons in preparing wills, mortgages, deeds, deeds of trust, or any other legal document.
2. Provide immigration consultation.
3. Provide legal advice.
4. Choose the appropriate notarial certificate to be placed on a document.

## Advertising Notary Public Services in a Language Other Than English

If a non-attorney notary advertises his or her services in a foreign language, the notary must also provide the same advertisement in English. The notice, which may be written or spoken, must be conspicuous and state:

> I AM NOT AN ATTORNEY LICENSED TO PRACTICE LAW IN THE STATE OF NORTH CAROLINA, AND I MAY NOT GIVE LEGAL ADVICE OR ACCEPT FEES FOR LEGAL ADVICE.

G.S. 10B-20(i).

## Posting Fees in English

If a notary charges a fee for notary services, the notary must post those fees in English at his or her regular place of business in a type font no smaller than 10 points. G.S. 10B-32.

# Certifying a True Copy or Notarizing or Authenticating a Photograph

A notary public possesses only three powers:

1. Taking acknowledgments
2. Taking verifications and proofs
3. Administering oaths and affirmations

A notary does not have the authority to certify true copies, authenticate photographs, or otherwise perform any other service not specifically set out by law. Although the Notary Act only authorizes three powers, North Carolina notaries may also inventory an abandoned safe deposit box and notarize a voter absentee ballot as discussed in Chapter 7.

# Using the Notary's Official Seal as an Endorsement for Anything

The notary's seal or stamp is his or her official emblem of having a valid commission and being authorized by the North Carolina Department of the Secretary of State to perform the notarial acts as prescribed by law. The notary must not place his or her seal on anything for other than a bona fide notarial act.

# 9
# Changes in Notary Status

Change of Address—G.S. 10B-50 . . . . . . . . . . . . . . . . . . . . . . . . . . . .86
Change of Name—G.S. 10B-51 . . . . . . . . . . . . . . . . . . . . . . . . . . . .86
Change of County—G.S. 10B-52 . . . . . . . . . . . . . . . . . . . . . . . . . . .88
Change of Both Name and County—G.S. 10B-53 . . . . . . . . . . . .89
Additional Obligations of Notaries . . . . . . . . . . . . . . . . . . . . . . . .89
Resignation—G.S. 10B-54 . . . . . . . . . . . . . . . . . . . . . . . . . . . . . . .90
Disposition of Seal—G.S. 10B-55 . . . . . . . . . . . . . . . . . . . . . . . . .90
Disposition of the Notary Journal . . . . . . . . . . . . . . . . . . . . . . . . .91

North Carolina notaries have a statutory obligation to notify the Department of the Secretary of State of any change of name, address, county of residence, employer, or phone number within 45 days of the effective date of the change. G.S. 10B-50, -51. Additionally, if the notary relocates outside of North Carolina but maintains employment in North Carolina, the notary must notify the Department within 45 days and may be commissioned in his or her county of employment. G.S. 10B-5(c). Notaries who relocate to another state and no longer work in North Carolina must resign their notary commission. G.S. 10B-54.

If the notary passes away, the notary's estate should notify the Department in writing and deliver the notary's seal as soon as reasonably possible before the estate closes. G.S. 10B-55. However, a personal representative who is not a notary and is not aware that the decedent was a commissioned notary is not required to comply with this provision but will be required in any enforcement proceeding to provide a statement under oath that he or she was unaware of the relative's status as a notary. G.S. 10B-55(c).

The Change of Status form can be accessed on the Department's website at **www.sosnc.gov** at **Forms** on the Notary Public home page.

All notices of a change in status must be signed and may be sent to the Secretary of State by fax, email, or certified mail, return receipt requested. In the case of email, the typed name on an email will satisfy the requirement of an electronic signature and will be acceptable.

Table 1 presents a quick reference guide for change of status.

## Change of Address—G.S. 10B-50

When a notary changes his or her residence, business, or any mailing address or telephone number, the notary shall send notification to the Department within 45 days of the change. The notice should include both the old and new addresses or telephone numbers. G.S. 10B-50.

## Change of Name—G.S. 10B-51

After a legal change of name, a notary must send a signed notice of the change to the Department within 45 days. The notice must include both the former name and the notary's new name.

The notary may continue to notarize in the notary's former name until he or she receives confirmation of the name change from the Department, takes a new oath of office at the

# Table 1. Quick Reference Guide for Change of Status

| Action | Form | Time Frame | Fee | Oath* |
|---|---|---|---|---|
| Name change | Name/Address Change Form | Within 45 days of name change | 0 | Yes |
| Address change not involving a county change | Name/Address Change Form | Within 45 days of address change | 0 | No |
| Name and address change not involving a county change | Name/Address Change Form | Within 45 days of name/address change | 0 | Yes |
| Name and address change that involves a county change | Reappointment Form | Within 45 days of name/county change | $50 | Yes |
| County change only (no name change) | Name/Address Change Form | Within 45 days of address/county change | 0 | No |
| Commission lapses for more than 1 year | Notary Public Course and Initial Application | N/A | $50 | Yes |
| Changes residence to another state or no longer works for a North Carolina employer | Resignation Letter and Seal sent by certified mail, return receipt requested, to the Notary Public Section | Immediately | 0 | N/A |
| Notary resigns or is no longer able to serve as a notary | Resignation Letter and Seal sent by certified mail, return receipt requested, to the Notary Public Section | Immediately | 0 | N/A |
| Notary's death | Estate delivers Notice of Death and Seal to the Department | Prior to the closing of the estate | 0 | N/A |

*The oath for a commission or re-commission under a new name and/or county is required to be taken in the register of deeds office in the commissioning county within 45 days of the issue date of the oath notification letter sent by the Department. The notary will also have to purchase a new seal to reflect the appropriate county and/or new name. Failure to take the oath of office within 45 days will render the notary commission inactive and may result in disciplinary action.

register of deeds office in the county of his or her commission, and obtains a new notary seal in his or her new name.

After receiving confirmation of the name change, the notary has 45 days from the effective date of the change to appear before the register of deeds and take the oath of office in the notary's new name. After completing these steps, the notary may begin notarizing in his or her new name.

Failure to take the oath of office within 45 days will render the notary commission inactive and may result in disciplinary action.

## Change of County—G.S. 10B-52

North Carolina notaries public have statewide jurisdiction and can notarize anywhere within the geographical boundaries of the state. Therefore, when a notary moves to a different county during the notary's commission term, he or she simply needs to notify the Department of the change of address. The notary continues to notarize using the same notary seal or stamp until his or her current commission expires.

Once the notary's commission has expired and the notary seeks to be re-commissioned, the notary simply completes the reappointment application listing his or her new county and submits it to the Department along with the applicable commission fee. Upon receiving the oath notification letter from the Department, the notary takes an oath of office at the register of deeds office in the new county within 45 days and obtains a new notary seal reflecting the new county of commission.

# Change of Both Name and County—G.S. 10B-53

Within 45 days after the legal change of a notary's name and a change in his or her county of commission, the notary must submit a reappointment application to the Department along with the applicable fee reflecting the change of name and county. Upon receiving the oath notification letter from the Department, the notary must take an oath of office at the register of deeds office in the new county within 45 days and obtain a new notary seal reflecting the new name and county of commission.

Failure to take the oath of office within 45 days will render the notary commission inactive and may result in disciplinary action.

The notary may continue to perform notarial acts under the notary's previous name and seal until the steps outlined above have been completed.

# Additional Obligations of Notaries

Notaries also are obliged to notify the Department of changes that may negatively impact their ability to hold the office of notary public, including the following:

- Conviction of a crime involving moral turpitude as described in Chapter 3
- Changes in the notary's ability to speak, read, and write the English language
- The finding or admission of liability in a civil lawsuit based upon the notary's deceit
- Revocation, suspension, restriction, or denial of a professional license by the State of North Carolina or any other state or nation
- A finding that the notary has engaged in official misconduct

- A finding or a charge that a notary has knowingly used false or misleading advertising in which the notary was represented as having powers, duties, rights, or privileges that a North Carolina notary, by law, does not possess
- A finding by the North Carolina State Bar or the courts of North Carolina or the bar or courts of any other state or nation that the notary has engaged in the unauthorized practice of law

18 NCAC 07B .0107.

## Resignation—G.S. 10B-54

Upon resignation the notary is required to send to the Secretary of State by fax, email, or certified mail, return receipt requested, a signed notice indicating the effective date of resignation.

Resignation is automatically triggered when a notary ceases to reside in or to maintain a regular place of work or business in this state or when the notary becomes permanently unable to perform his or her notarial duties. When a notary resigns his or her commission, the notary must also deliver his or her notary seal(s) to the Secretary of State by certified mail, return receipt requested.

## Disposition of Seal—G.S. 10B-55

When a notary commission is resigned or revoked, the notary is required to deliver his or her seal to the Secretary of State within 45 days of the resignation or revocation by certified mail, return receipt requested.

The Secretary of State will take measures to destroy the notary seal to ensure that it will not be used.

A notary whose commission has expired and whose previous commission or application was not revoked or denied is not required to turn his or her seal in to the Secretary of State if the notary applies to be re-commissioned within three months of his or her commission expiration.

If a notary dies during his or her commission term or before being able to properly dispose of the notary seal as described in this section, the notary's estate is responsible for notifying the Department in writing of the notary's death and delivering the seal to the Secretary of State for destruction.

## Disposition of the Notary Journal

The Department recommends that notaries maintain their notary journals for a minimum of 10 years after the expiration of their final commission. However, notaries may determine to keep possession of their notary journals for a much longer period of time based on the business practices of their specific industry.

# Appendix A: North Carolina General Statutes

Chapter 10B.

Notaries.

Article 1.

Notary Public Act.

Part 1. General Provisions.

§ 10B-1. Short title.

This Article is the "Notary Public Act" and may be cited by that name.

§ 10B-2. Purposes.

This Chapter shall be construed and applied to advance its underlying purposes, which are the following:

(1) To promote, serve, and protect the public interests.

(2) To simplify, clarify, and modernize the law governing notaries.

(3) To prevent fraud and forgery.

(4) To foster ethical conduct among notaries.

(5) To enhance interstate recognition of notarial acts.

(6) To integrate procedures for traditional paper and electronic notarial acts.

## § 10B-3. Definitions.

The following definitions apply in this Chapter:

(1) Acknowledgment.—A notarial act in which a notary certifies that at a single time and place all of the following occurred:

    a. An individual appeared in person before the notary and presented a record.

    b. The individual was personally known to the notary or identified by the notary through satisfactory evidence.

    c. The individual did either of the following:

        i. Indicated to the notary that the signature on the record was the individual's signature.

        ii. Signed the record while in the physical presence of the notary and while being personally observed signing the record by the notary.

(2) Affirmation.—A notarial act which is legally equivalent to an oath and in which a notary certifies that at a single time and place all of the following occurred:

    a. An individual appeared in person before the notary.

    b. The individual was personally known to the notary or identified by the notary through satisfactory evidence.

    c. The individual made a vow of truthfulness on penalty of perjury, based on personal honor and without invoking a deity or using any form of the word "swear".

(3) Attest or attestation.—The completion of a certificate by a notary who has performed a notarial act.

(4) Commission.—The empowerment to perform notarial acts and the written evidence of authority to perform those acts.

(5) Credible witness.—An individual who is personally known to the notary and to whom all of the following also apply:

    a. The notary believes the individual to be honest and reliable for the purpose of confirming to the notary the identity of another individual.

    b. The notary believes the individual is not a party to or beneficiary of the transaction.

(6) Department.—The North Carolina Department of the Secretary of State.

(7) Director.—The Division Director for the North Carolina Department of the Secretary of State Notary Public Section.

(8) Jurat.—A notary's certificate evidencing the administration of an oath or affirmation.

(9) Moral turpitude.—Conduct contrary to expected standards of honesty, morality, or integrity.

(10) Nickname.—A descriptive, familiar, or shortened form of a proper name.

(11) Notarial act, notary act, and notarization.—The act of taking an acknowledgment, taking a verification or proof or administering an oath or affirmation that a notary is empowered to perform under G.S. 10B-20(a).

(12) Notarial certificate and certificate.—The portion of a notarized record that is completed by the notary, bears the notary's signature and seal, and states the facts attested by the notary in a particular notarization.

(13) Notary public and notary.—A person commissioned to perform notarial acts under this Chapter. A notary is a public officer of the State of North Carolina and shall act in full and strict compliance with this act.

(14) Oath.—A notarial act which is legally equivalent to an affirmation and in which a notary certifies that at a single time and place all of the following occurred:

    a. An individual appeared in person before the notary.

    b. The individual was personally known to the notary or identified by the notary through satisfactory evidence.

    c. The individual made a vow of truthfulness on penalty of perjury while invoking a deity or using any form of the word "swear".

(15) Official misconduct.—Either of the following:

    a. A notary's performance of a prohibited act or failure to perform a mandated act set forth in this Chapter or any other law in connection with notarization.

    b. A notary's performance of a notarial act in a manner found by the Secretary to be negligent or against the public interest.

(16) Personal appearance and appear in person before a notary.—An individual and a notary are in close physical proximity to one another so that they may freely see and communicate with one another and exchange records back and forth during the notarization process.

(17) Personal knowledge or personally know.— Familiarity with an individual resulting from interactions with that individual over a period of

time sufficient to eliminate every reasonable doubt that the individual has the identity claimed.

(18) Principal.—One of the following:

a.  In the case of an acknowledgment, the individual whose identity and due execution of a record is being certified by the notary.

b.  In the case of a verification or proof, the individual other than a subscribing witness, whose:

   i.  Identity and due execution of the record is being proven; or

   ii.  Signature is being identified as genuine.

c.  In the case of an oath or affirmation, the individual who makes a vow of truthfulness on penalty of perjury.

(19) Record.—Information that is inscribed on a tangible medium and called a traditional or paper record.

(20) Regular place of work or business.—A location, office or other workspace, where an individual regularly spends all or part of the individual's work time.

(21) Revocation.—The cancellation of the notary's commission stated in the order of revocation.

(22) Satisfactory evidence.—Identification of an individual based on either of the following:

a.  At least one current document issued by a federal, state, or federal or state-recognized tribal government agency bearing the photographic image of the individual's face and either the signature or a physical description of the individual.

b.  The oath or affirmation of one credible witness who personally knows the individual seeking to be identified.

(23) Seal or stamp.—A device for affixing on a paper record an image containing a notary's name, the words "notary public," and other information as required in G.S. 10B-37.

(24) Secretary.—The North Carolina Secretary of State or the Secretary's designee.

(25) Repealed by Session Laws 2006-59, s. 1, effective October 1, 2006, except as otherwise set forth in the act, and applicable to notarial acts performed on or after October 1, 2006.

(26) Subscribing witness.—A person who signs a record for the purpose of being a witness to the principal's execution of the record or to the principal's acknowledgment of his or her execution of the record. A subscribing witness may give proof of the execution of the record as provided in subdivision (28) of this section.

(27) Suspension and restriction.—The termination of a notary's commission for a period of time stated in an order of restriction or suspension. The terms "restriction" or "suspension" or a combination of both terms shall be used synonymously.

(28) Verification or proof.—A notarial act in which a notary certifies that all of the following occurred:

   a.  An individual appeared in person before the notary.

   b.  The individual was personally known to the notary or identified by the notary through satisfactory evidence.

   c.  The individual was not a party to or beneficiary of the transaction.

   d.  The individual took an oath or gave an affirmation and testified to one of the following:

      i.  The individual is a subscribing witness and the principal who signed the record

did so while being personally observed
by the subscribing witness.

ii.   The individual is a subscribing witness
and the principal who signed the record
acknowledged his or her signature to the
subscribing witness.

iii.   The individual recognized either the signature on the record of the principal or
the signature on the record of the subscribing witness and the signature was
genuine.

§ 10B-4: Reserved for future codification purposes.


# Part 2. Commissioning.


## § 10B-5. Qualifications.

(a)   Except as provided in subsection (d) of this section, the
Secretary shall commission as a notary any qualified person
who submits an application in accordance with this Chapter.

(b)   A person qualified for a notarial commission shall meet
all of the following requirements:

(1)   Be at least 18 years of age or legally emancipated
as defined in Article 35 of Chapter 7B of the
General Statutes.

(2)   Reside or have a regular place of work or business
in this State.

(3)   Reside legally in the United States.

(4)   Speak, read, and write the English language.

(5)   Possess a high school diploma or equivalent.

(6)   Pass the course of instruction described in this
Article, unless the person is a licensed member of
the North Carolina State Bar.

(7) Purchase and keep as a reference the most recent manual approved by the Secretary that describes the duties and authority of notaries public.

(8) Submit an application containing no significant misstatement or omission of fact. The application form shall be provided by the Secretary and be available at the register of deeds office in each county. Every application shall include the signature of the applicant written with pen and ink, and the signature shall be acknowledged by the applicant before a person authorized to administer oaths.

(9) Repealed by Session Laws 2013-204, s. 1, effective July 1, 2013.

(c) The notary shall be commissioned in his or her county of residence, unless the notary is not a North Carolina resident, in which case he or she shall be commissioned in the county of his or her employment or business.

(d) The Secretary may deny an application for commission or recommission if any of the following apply to an applicant:

(1) Submission of an incomplete application or an application containing material misstatement or omission of fact.

(2) The applicant's conviction or plea of admission or nolo contendere to a felony or any crime involving dishonesty or moral turpitude. In no case may a commission be issued to an applicant within 10 years after release from prison, probation, or parole, whichever is later.

(3) A finding or admission of liability against the applicant in a civil lawsuit based on the applicant's deceit.

(4) The revocation, suspension, restriction, or denial of a notarial commission or professional license by this or any other state or nation. In no case may a

commission be issued to an applicant within five years after the completion of all conditions of any disciplinary order.

(5) A finding that the applicant has engaged in official misconduct, whether or not disciplinary action resulted.

(6) An applicant knowingly using false or misleading advertising in which the applicant as a notary represents that the applicant has powers, duties, rights, or privileges that the applicant does not possess by law.

(7) A finding by a state bar or court that the applicant has engaged in the unauthorized practice of law.

## § 10B-6. Application for commission.

Every application for a notary commission shall be made on paper with original signatures, or in another form determined by the Secretary, and shall include all of the following:

(1) A statement of the applicant's personal qualifications as required by this Chapter.

(2) A certificate or signed statement by the instructor evidencing successful completion of the course of instruction as required by this Chapter.

(3) A notarized declaration of the applicant, as required by this Chapter.

(4) Any other information that the Secretary deems appropriate.

(5) The application fee required by this Chapter.

## § 10B-7. Statement of personal qualification.

(a) The application for a notary commission shall include at least all of the following:

(1) The applicant's full legal name and the name to be used for commissioning, excluding nicknames.

(2) The applicant's date of birth.

(3) The mailing address for the applicant's residence, the street address for the applicant's residence, and the telephone number for the applicant's residence.

(4) The applicant's county of residence.

(5) The name of the applicant's employer, the street and mailing address for the applicant's employer, and telephone number for the applicant's employer.

(6) The applicant's last four digits of the applicant's social security number.

(7) The applicant's personal and business e-mail addresses.

(8) A declaration that the applicant is a citizen of the United States or proof of the applicant's legal residency in this country.

(9) A declaration that the applicant can speak, read, and writes in the English language.

(10) A complete listing of any issuances, denials, revocations, suspensions, restrictions, and resignations of a notarial commission, professional license, or public office involving the applicant in this or any other state or nation.

(11) A complete listing of any criminal convictions of the applicant, including any pleas of admission or nolo contendere, in this or any other state or nation.

(12) A complete listing of any civil findings or admissions of fault or liability regarding the applicant's activities as a notary, in this or any other state or nation.

(b) The information provided in an application that relates to subdivisions (2), (3), (6), and (7) of subsection (a) of this section shall be considered confidential information and shall not be subject to disclosure under Chapter 132 of the General Statutes.

## § 10B-8. Course of study and examination.

(a)   Every applicant for an initial notary commission shall, within the three months preceding application, take a course of classroom instruction of not less than six hours approved by the Secretary and take a written examination approved by the Secretary. An applicant must answer at least eighty percent (80%) of the questions correctly in order to pass the exam. This subsection shall not apply to a licensed member of the North Carolina State Bar.

(b)   Every applicant for recommissioning shall pass a written examination approved by and administered by or under the direction of the Secretary, unless the person is a licensed member of the North Carolina State Bar.

(c)   The content of the course of instruction and the written examinations shall be notarial laws, procedures, and ethics.

(d)   The Secretary may charge such fees as are reasonably necessary to pay the cost associated with developing and administering examinations permitted by this Chapter and for conducting the training of notaries and notary instructors.

## § 10B-9. Length of term and jurisdiction.

A person commissioned under this Chapter may perform notarial acts in any part of this State for a term of five years, unless the commission is earlier revoked or resigned. No commissions shall be effective prior to the administration of the oath of office. Any notarial acts performed before the administration of the oath of office, either the original commissioning or recommissioning, are invalid.

## § 10B-10. Commission; oath of office.

(a)   If the Secretary grants a commission to an applicant, the Secretary shall notify the appointee and shall instruct the appointee regarding the proper procedure for taking the oath at the register of deeds office in the county of the appointee's commissioning.

(b)  The appointee shall appear before the register of deeds no later than 45 days after commissioning and shall be duly qualified by taking the general oath of office prescribed in G.S. 11-11 and the oath prescribed for officers in G.S. 11-7.

(c)  After the appointee qualifies by taking the oath of office required under subsection (b) of this section, the register of deeds shall place the notary record in a book designated for that purpose, or the notary record may be recorded in the Consolidated Document Book and indexed in the Consolidated Real Property Index under the notary's name in the grantor index. The notary record may be kept in electronic format so long as the signature of the notary public may be viewed and printed. The notary record shall contain the name and the signature of the notary as commissioned, the effective date and expiration date of the commission, the date the oath was administered, and the date of any restriction, suspension, revocation, or resignation. The record shall constitute the official record of the qualification of notaries public.

(d)  The register of deeds shall deliver the commission to the notary following completion of the requirements of this section and shall notify the Secretary of the delivery.

(e)  If the appointee does not appear before the register of deeds within 45 days of commissioning, the register of deeds must return the commission to the Secretary, and the appointee must reapply for commissioning. If the appointee reapplies within one year of the granting of the commission, the Secretary may waive the educational requirements of this Chapter.

§ 10B-11.  Recommissioning.

(a)  A commissioned notary may apply for recommissioning no earlier than 10 weeks prior to the expiration date of the notary's commission.

(b)   A notary whose commission has not expired must comply with the following requirements to be recommissioned:

(1)   Submit a new application meeting the requirements of G.S. 10B-6, except for G.S. 10B-6(2).

(2)   Meet all the requirements of G.S. 10B-5(b), except for G.S. 10B-5(b)(5), (6), and (9).

(3)   Achieve a passing score on the written examination required under G.S. 10B-8(b). This requirement does not apply if the notary is a licensed member of the North Carolina State Bar, or if the notary has been continuously commissioned in North Carolina since July 10, 1991, and has never been disciplined by the Secretary.

(c)   An individual may apply for recommissioning within one year after the expiration of the individual's commission. The individual must comply with the requirement of subsection (b) of this section. The individual must also fulfill the educational requirement under G.S. 10B-8(a), unless the Secretary waives that requirement.

§ 10B-12. Notarized declaration.

The application for a notary public commission shall contain the following declaration to be executed by each applicant under oath:

Declaration of Applicant

I, _____ (name of applicant), solemnly swear or affirm under penalty of perjury that the information in this application is true, complete, and correct; that I understand the official duties and responsibilities of a notary public in this State, as described in the statutes; and that I will perform to

the best of my ability all notarial acts in accordance
with the law.

_____

(signature of applicant)

§ 10B-13. Application fee.

Every applicant for a notary commission shall pay to the
Secretary a nonrefundable application fee of fifty dollars
($50.00).

§ 10B-14. Instructor's certification.

(a)   The course of study required by G.S. 10B-5(b) shall be
taught by an instructor certified under rules adopted by the
Secretary. An instructor must meet the following requirements
to be certified to teach a course of study for notaries public:

(1)   Complete and pass an instructor certification
course of not less than six hours taught by
the Director or other person approved by the
Secretary.

(2)   Have at least one year of active experience as a
notary public.

(3)   Maintain a current commission as a notary public.

(4)   Possess the current notary public guidebook.

(5)   Pay a nonrefundable fee of fifty dollars ($50.00).

(b)   Certification to teach a course of study for notaries shall be effective for two years. A certification may be
renewed by passing a recertification course taught by the
Director or other person approved by the Secretary and by
paying a nonrefundable fee of fifty dollars ($50.00).

(c)   The following individuals may be certified to teach
a course of study for notaries public without paying the fee
required by this section, and they may renew their certification
without paying the renewal fee, so long as they remain actively
employed in the capacities named:

(1)   Registers of deeds.

(2)  Clerks of court.

(3)  The Director and other duly authorized employees of the Secretary.

(d)  Former registers of deeds and clerks of court who have been certified as notary public instructors must apply for commissioning as a notary public but are exempt from the education requirements of G.S. 10B-8 after successful completion of an examination administered by the Secretary.

(e)  Assistant and deputy registers of deeds and assistant and deputy clerks of court must have a regular notary commission prior to receiving a certification or recertification as a notary public instructor.

(f)  The Secretary may suspend or revoke the certification of a notary instructor for violating the provisions of this Chapter or any of the administrative rules implementing it.


## Part 3. Notarial Acts, Powers, and Limitations.


§ 10B-20.  Powers and limitations.

(a)  A notary may perform any of the following notarial acts:

(1)  Acknowledgments.

(2)  Oaths and affirmations.

(3)  Repealed by Session Laws 2006-59, s. 6, effective October 1, 2006, and except as otherwise set forth in the act, applicable to notarial acts performed on or after October 1, 2006.

(4)  Verifications or proofs.

(b)  A notarial act shall be attested by all of the following:

(1)  The signature of the notary, exactly as shown on the notary's commission.

(2)  The legible appearance of the notary's name exactly as shown on the notary's commission.

The legible appearance of the name may be
ascertained from the notary's typed or printed
name near the notary's signature or from
elsewhere in the notarial certificate or from the
notary's seal if the name is legible.

(3) The clear and legible appearance of the notary's
stamp or seal.

(4) A statement of the date the notary's commission
expires. The statement of the date that the
notary's commission expires may appear in the
notary's stamp or seal or elsewhere in the notarial
certificate.

(c) A notary shall not perform a notarial act if any of the
following apply:

(1) The principal or subscribing witness is not in the
notary's presence at the time the notarial act
is performed. However, nothing in this Chapter
shall require a notary to complete the notarial
certificate attesting to the notarial act in the
presence of the principal or subscribing witness.

(2) The principal or subscribing witness is not
personally known to the notary or identified by the
notary through satisfactory evidence.

(2a) The credible witness is not personally known to
the notary.

(3), (4) Repealed by Session Laws 2006-59, s. 8, effective
October 1, 2006, and except as otherwise set
forth in the act, applicable to notarial acts
performed on or after October 1, 2006.

(5) The notary is a signer of, party to, or beneficiary
of the record, that is to be notarized. However,
a disqualification under this subdivision shall
not apply to a notary who is named in a record
solely as (i) the trustee in a deed of trust, (ii) the
drafter of the record, (iii) the person to whom a

registered document should be mailed or sent after recording, or (iv) the attorney for a party to the record, so long as the notary is not also a party to the record individually or in some other representative or fiduciary capacity. A notary who is an employee of a party shall not be disqualified under this subdivision solely because of the notary's employment by a party to the record or solely because the notary owns stock in a party to the record.

(6) The notary will receive directly from a transaction connected with the notarial act any commission, fee, advantage, right, title, interest, cash, property, or other consideration exceeding in value the fees specified in G.S. 10B-31, other than fees or other consideration paid for services rendered by a licensed attorney, a licensed real estate broker or salesperson, a motor vehicle dealer, or a banker.

(d) A notary may certify the affixation of a signature by mark on a record presented for notarization if:

(1) The mark is affixed in the presence of the notary;

(2) The notary writes below the mark: "Mark affixed by (name of signer by mark) in presence of undersigned notary"; and

(3) The notary notarizes the signature by performing an acknowledgment, oath or affirmation, jurat, or verification or proof.

(e) If a principal is physically unable to sign or make a mark on a record presented for notarization, that principal may designate another person as his or her designee, who shall be a disinterested party, to sign on the principal's behalf pursuant to the following procedure:

(1) The principal directs the designee to sign the record in the presence of the notary and two witnesses unaffected by the record;

(2) The designee signs the principal's name in the presence of the principal, the notary, and the two witnesses;

(3) Both witnesses sign their own names to the record near the principal's signature;

(4) The notary writes below the principal's signature: "Signature affixed by designee in the presence of (names and addresses of principal and witnesses)"; and

(5) The notary notarizes the signature through an acknowledgment, oath or affirmation, jurat, or verification or proof.

(f)  A notarial act performed in another jurisdiction in compliance with the laws of that jurisdiction is valid to the same extent as if it had been performed by a notary commissioned under this Chapter if the notarial act is performed by a notary public of that jurisdiction or by any person authorized to perform notarial acts in that jurisdiction under the laws of that jurisdiction, the laws of this State, or federal law.

(g)  Persons authorized by federal law or regulation to perform notarial acts may perform the acts for persons serving in or with the Armed Forces of the United States, their spouses, and their dependents.

(h)  The Secretary and register of deeds in the county in which a notary qualified may certify to the commission of the notary.

(i)  A notary public who is not an attorney licensed to practice law in this State who advertises the person's services as a notary public in a language other than English, by radio, television, signs, pamphlets, newspapers, other written communication, or in any other manner, shall post or otherwise include with the advertisement the notice set forth in this subsection in English and in the language used for the advertisement. The notice shall be of conspicuous size, if in writing, and shall state:

"I AM NOT AN ATTORNEY LICENSED TO PRACTICE LAW IN THE STATE OF NORTH CAROLINA, AND I MAY NOT GIVE LEGAL ADVICE OR ACCEPT FEES FOR LEGAL ADVICE." If the advertisement is by radio or television, the statement may be modified but must include substantially the same message.

(j)   A notary public who is not an attorney licensed to practice law in this State is prohibited from representing or advertising that the notary public is an "immigration consultant" or expert on immigration matters unless the notary public is an accredited representative of an organization recognized by the Board of Immigration Appeals pursuant to Title 8, Part 292, section 2(a-e) of the Code of Federal Regulations (8 C.F.R. § 292.2(a-e)).

(k)   A notary public who is not an attorney licensed to practice law in this State is prohibited from rendering any service that constitutes the unauthorized practice of law. A nonattorney notary shall not assist another person in drafting, completing, selecting, or understanding a record or transaction requiring a notarial act.

(l)   A notary public required to comply with the provisions of subsection (i) of this section shall prominently post at the notary public's place of business a schedule of fees established by law, which a notary public may charge. The fee schedule shall be written in English and in the non-English language in which the notary services were solicited and shall contain the notice required in subsection (i) of this section, unless the notice is otherwise prominently posted at the notary public's place of business.

(m)   If notarial certificate wording is not provided or indicated for a record, a notary who is not also a licensed attorney shall not determine the type of notarial act or certificate to be used. This does not prohibit a notary from offering the selection of certificate forms recognized in this Chapter or as otherwise authorized by law.

(n)   A notary shall not claim to have powers, qualifications, rights, or privileges that the office of notary does not provide, including the power to counsel on immigration matters.

(o)   Before signing a notarial certificate and except as provided in this subsection, a notary shall cross out or mark through all blank lines or spaces in the certificate. However:

(1)   Notwithstanding the provisions of this section, a notary shall not be required to complete, cross out, or mark through blank lines or spaces in the notary certificate form provided for in G.S. 47-43 indicating when and where a power of attorney is recorded if that recording information is not known to the notary at the time the notary completes and signs the certificate;

(2)   A notary's failure to cross out or mark through blank lines or spaces in a notarial certificate shall not affect the sufficiency, validity, or enforceability of the certificate or the related record; and

(3)   A notary's failure to cross out or mark through blank lines or spaces in a notarial certificate shall not be grounds for a register of deeds to refuse to accept a record for registration.

§ 10B-21. Notaries ex officio.

(a)   The clerks of the superior court may act as notaries public in their several counties by virtue of their offices as clerks and may certify their notarial acts only under the seals of their respective courts. Assistant and deputy clerks of superior court, by virtue of their offices, may perform the following notarial acts and may certify these notarial acts only under the seals of their respective courts:

(1)   Oaths and affirmations.

(2)   Verifications or proofs.

Upon completion of the course of study provided for in G.S. 10B-5(b), assistant and deputy clerks of superior court may, by virtue of their offices, perform all other notarial acts and may certify these notarial acts only under the seals of their respective courts. A course of study attended only by assistant and deputy clerks of superior court may be taught at any mutually convenient location agreed to by the Secretary and the Administrative Office of the Courts.

(b) Registers of deeds may act as notaries public in their several counties by virtue of their offices as registers of deeds and may certify their notarial acts only under the seals of their respective offices. Assistant and deputy registers of deeds, by virtue of their offices, may perform the following notarial acts and may certify these notarial acts only under the seals of their respective offices:

(1) Oaths and affirmations.

(2) Verifications or proofs.

Upon completion of the course of study provided for in G.S. 10B-5(b), assistant and deputy registers of deeds may, by virtue of their offices, perform all other notarial acts and may certify these notarial acts only under the seals of their respective offices. A course of study attended only by assistant and deputy registers of deeds may be taught at any mutually convenient location agreed to by the Secretary and the North Carolina Association of Registers of Deeds.

(c) The Director may act as a notary public by virtue of the Director's employment in the Department of the Secretary and may certify a notarial act performed in that capacity under the seal of the Secretary.

(d) Unless otherwise provided by law, a person designated a notary public by this section may charge a fee for a notarial act performed in accordance with G.S. 10B-31. The fee authorized by this section is payable to the governmental unit or agency by whom the person is employed.

(e) Nothing in this section shall authorize a person to act as a notary public other than in the performance of the official duties of the person's office unless the person complies fully with the requirements of G.S. 10B-5.

## § 10B-22. False certificate; foreign language certificates.

(a)  A notary shall not execute a notarial certificate containing information known or believed by the notary to be false.

(b)  A notary shall not execute a certificate that is not written in the English language. A notary may execute a certificate written in the English language that accompanies a record written in another language, which record may include a translation of the notarial certificate into the other language. In those instances, the notary shall execute only the English language certificate.

## § 10B-23. Improper records.

(a)  A notary shall not notarize a signature on a record without a notarial certificate indicating what type of notarial act was performed. However, a notary may administer an oath or affirmation without completing a jurat.

(b)  A notary shall neither certify, notarize, nor authenticate a photograph. A notary may notarize an affidavit regarding and attached to a photograph.

## § 10B-24. Testimonials.

A notary shall not use the official notary title or seal in a manner intended to endorse, promote, denounce, or oppose any product, service, contest, candidate, or other offering. This section does not prohibit a notary public from performing a notarial act upon a record executed by another individual.

# Part 4. Fees.

## § 10B-30. Imposition and waiver of fees.

(a)  For performing a notarial act, a notary may charge up to the maximum fee specified in this Chapter.

(b)  A notary shall not discriminatorily condition the fee for a notarial act on any attribute of the principal that would constitute unlawful discrimination.

(c)   Nothing in this Chapter shall compel a notary to charge a fee.

(d)   A notary may not charge any fee for witnessing and affixing a notarial seal to an absentee ballot application or certificate under G.S. 163-231.

§ 10B-31.  Fees for notarial acts.

The maximum fees that may be charged by a notary for notarial acts are as follows:

(1)   For acknowledgments, jurats, verifications or proofs, five dollars ($5.00) per principal signature.

(2)   For oaths or affirmations without a signature, five dollars ($5.00) per person, except for an oath or affirmation administered to a credible witness to vouch for the identity of a principal or subscribing witness.

§ 10B-32.  Notice of fees.

Notaries who charge for their notarial services shall conspicuously display in their places of business, or present to each principal outside their places of business, an English-language schedule of fees for notarial acts. No part of any notarial fee schedule shall be printed in smaller than 10-point type.

## Part 5. Signature and Seal.

§ 10B-35.  Official signature.

When notarizing a paper record, a notary shall sign by hand in ink on the notarial certificate. The notary shall comply with the requirements of G.S. 10B-20(b)(1) and (b)(2). The notary shall affix the official signature only after the notarial act is performed. The notary shall not sign a paper record using the facsimile stamp or an electronic or other printing method.

## § 10B-36. Official seal.

(a)  A notary shall keep an official seal or stamp that is the exclusive property of the notary. The notary shall keep the seal in a secure location. A notary shall not allow another person to use or possess the seal, and shall not surrender the seal to the notary's employer upon termination of employment.

(b)  The seal shall be affixed only after the notarial act is performed. The notary shall place the image or impression of the seal near the notary's signature on every paper record notarized. The seal and the notary's signature shall appear on the same page of a record as the text of the notarial certificate.

(c)  A notary shall do the following within 10 days of discovering that the notary's seal has been lost or stolen:

(1)  Inform the appropriate law enforcement agency in the case of theft or vandalism.

(2)  Notify the appropriate register of deeds and the Secretary in writing and signed in the official name in which he or she was commissioned.

(d)  As soon as is reasonably practicable after resignation, revocation, or expiration of a notary commission, or death of the notary, the seal shall be delivered to the Secretary for disposal.

## § 10B-37. Seal image.

(a)  A notary shall affix the notary's official seal near the notary's official signature on the notarial certificate of a record.

(b)  A notary's official seal shall include all of the following elements:

(1)  The notary's name exactly as commissioned.

(2)  The words "Notary Public".

(3)  The county of commissioning, including the word "County" or the abbreviation "Co.".

(4)  The words "North Carolina" or the abbreviation "N.C." or "NC".

(c) The notary seal may be either circular or rectangular in shape. Upon receiving a commission or a recommission on or after October 1, 2006, a notary shall not use a circular seal that is less than 1 1/2 inches, nor more than 2 inches in diameter. The rectangular seal shall not be over 1 inch high and 2 1/2 inches long. The perimeter of the seal shall contain a border that is visible when impressed.

(c1) Alterations to any information contained within the seal as embossed or stamped on the record are prohibited.

(d) A notarial seal, as it appears on a record, may contain the permanently imprinted, handwritten, or typed date the notary's commission expires.

(e) Any reference in the General Statutes to the seal of a notary shall include the stamp of a notary, and any reference to the stamp of a notary shall include the seal of the notary.

(f) The failure of a notarial seal to comply with the requirements of this section shall not affect the sufficiency, validity, or enforceability of the notarial certificate, but shall constitute a violation of the notary's duties.

## Part 6. Certificate Forms.

§ 10B-40. Notarial certificates in general.

(a) A notary shall not make or give a notarial certificate unless the notary has either personal knowledge or satisfactory evidence of the identity of the principal or, if applicable, the subscribing witness.

(a1) By making or giving a notarial certificate, whether or not stated in the certificate, a notary certifies as follows:

    (1) As to an acknowledgment, all those things described in G.S. 10B-3(1).

    (2) As to an affirmation, all those things described in G.S. 10B-3(2).

(3) As to an oath, all those things described in G.S. 10B-3(14).

(4) As to a verification or proof, all those things described in G.S. 10B-3(28).

(a2) In addition to the certifications under subsection (a1) of this section, by making or giving a notarial certificate, whether or not stated in the certificate, a notary certifies to all of the following:

(1) At the time the notarial act was performed and the notarial certificate was signed by the notary, the notary was lawfully commissioned, the notary's commission had neither expired nor been suspended, the notarial act was performed within the geographic limits of the notary's commission, and the notarial act was performed in accordance with the provision of this Chapter.

(2) If the notarial certificate is for an acknowledgment or the administration of an oath or affirmation, the person whose signature was notarized did not appear in the judgment of the notary to be incompetent, lacking in understanding of the nature and consequences of the transaction requiring the notarial act, or acting involuntarily, under duress, or undue influence.

(3) The notary was not prohibited from acting under G.S. 10-20(c).

(a3) The inclusion of additional information in a notarial certificate, including the representative or fiduciary capacity in which a person signed or the means a notary used to identify a principal, shall not invalidate an otherwise sufficient notarial certificate.

(b) A notarial certificate for the acknowledgment taken by a notary of a principal who is an individual acting in his or her own right or who is an individual acting in a representative or fiduciary capacity is sufficient and shall be accepted in this

State if it is substantially in the form set forth in G.S. 10B-41, if it is substantially in a form otherwise prescribed by the laws of this State, or if it includes all of the following:

(1) Identifies the state and county in which the acknowledgment occurred.

(2) Names the principal who appeared in person before the notary.

(3) Repealed by Session Laws 2006-59, s. 18, effective October 1, 2006, and except as otherwise set forth in the act, applicable to notarial acts performed on or after October 1, 2006.

(4) Indicates that the principal appeared in person before the notary and the principal acknowledged that he or she signed the record.

(5) States the date of the acknowledgment.

(6) Contains the signature and seal or stamp of the notary who took the acknowledgment.

(7) States the notary's commission expiration date.

(c) A notarial certificate for the verification or proof of the signature of a principal by a subscribing witness taken by a notary is sufficient and shall be accepted in this State if it is substantially in the form set forth in G.S. 10B-42, if it is substantially in a form otherwise prescribed by the laws of this State, or if it includes all of the following:

(1) Identifies the state and county in which the verification or proof occurred.

(2) Names the subscribing witness who appeared in person before the notary.

(3) Repealed by Session Laws 2006-59, s. 18, effective October 1, 2006.

(4) Names the principal whose signature on the record is to be verified or proven.

(5) Indicates that the subscribing witness certified to the notary under oath or by affirmation that the subscribing witness is not a party to or

> beneficiary of the transaction, signed the record as a subscribing witness, and either (i) witnessed the principal sign the record, or (ii) witnessed the principal acknowledge the principal's signature on the record.

(6) States the date of the verification or proof.

(7) Contains the signature and seal or stamp of the notary who took the verification or proof.

(8) States the notary's commission expiration date.

(c1) A notarial certificate for the verification or proof of the signature of a principal or a subscribing witness by a non-subscribing witness taken by a notary is sufficient and shall be accepted in this State if it is substantially in the form set forth in G.S. 10B-42.1, if it is substantially in a form otherwise prescribed by the laws of this State, or if it includes all of the following:

(1) Identifies the state and county in which the verification or proof occurred.

(2) Names the nonsubscribing witness who appeared in person before the notary.

(3) Names the principal or subscribing witness whose signature on the record is to be verified or proven.

(4) Indicates that the nonsubscribing witness certified to the notary under oath or by affirmation that the nonsubscribing witness is not a party to or beneficiary of the transaction and that the nonsubscribing witness recognizes the signature of either the principal or the subscribing witness and that the signature is genuine.

(5) States the date of the verification or proof.

(6) Contains the signature and seal or stamp of the notary who took the verification or proof.

(7) States the notary's commission expiration date.

(d) A notarial certificate for an oath or affirmation taken by a notary is sufficient and shall be accepted in this State if it is substantially in the form set forth in G.S. 10B-43, if it is substantially in a form otherwise prescribed by the laws of this State, or if it includes all of the following:

(1) Repealed by Session Laws 2006-59, s. 18, effective October 1, 2006.

(2) Names the principal who appeared in person before the notary unless the name of the principal otherwise is clear from the record itself.

(3) Repealed by Session Laws 2006-59, s. 18, effective October 1, 2006.

(4) Indicates that the principal who appeared in person before the notary signed the record in question and certified to the notary under oath or by affirmation as to the truth of the matters stated in the record.

(5) States the date of the oath or affirmation.

(6) Contains the signature and seal or stamp of the notary who took the oath or affirmation.

(7) States the notary's commission expiration date.

(e) Any notarial certificate made in another jurisdiction shall be sufficient in this State if it is made in accordance with federal law or the laws of the jurisdiction where the notarial certificate is made.

(f) On records to be filed, registered, recorded, or delivered in another state or jurisdiction of the United States, a North Carolina notary may complete any notarial certificate that may be required in that other state or jurisdiction.

(g) Nothing in this Chapter shall be deemed to authorize the use of a notarial certificate authorized by this Part in place of or as an alternative to a notarial certificate required by any other provision of the General Statutes outside of Chapter 47 of the General Statutes that prescribes the specific form or content for a notarial certificate including G.S. 31-11.6, Chapter 32A of the General Statutes, and G.S. 90-321. However, any statute that permits or requires the use of a notarial certificate contained within Chapter 47 of the General Statutes may also be satisfied by the use of a notarial certificate permitted by this Part. Any form of acknowledgment or probate authorized under Chapter 47 of the General Statutes shall be conclusively deemed in compliance with the requirements of this section.

(h) If an individual signs a record and purports to be acting in a representative or fiduciary capacity, that individual is also deemed to represent to the notary that he or she is signing the record with proper authority to do so and also is signing the record on behalf of the person or entity represented and identified therein or in the fiduciary capacity indicated therein. In performing a notarial act in relation to an individual described under this subsection, a notary is under no duty to verify whether the individual acted in a representative or fiduciary capacity or, if so, whether the individual was duly authorized so to do. A notarial certificate may include any of the following:

(1)   A statement that an individual signed a record in a particular representative or fiduciary capacity.

(2)   A statement that the individual who signed the record in a representative or fiduciary capacity had due authority so to do.

(3)   A statement identifying the represented person or entity or the fiduciary capacity.

§ 10B-41. Notarial certificate for an acknowledgment.

(a)   When properly completed by a notary, a notarial certificate that substantially complies with the following form may be used and shall be sufficient under the law of this State to satisfy the requirements for a notarial certificate for the acknowledgment of a principal who is an individual acting in his or her own right or who is an individual acting in a representative or fiduciary capacity. The authorization of the form in this section does not preclude the use of other forms.

_____ County, North Carolina

I certify that the following person(s) personally appeared before me this day, each acknowledging to me that he or she signed the foregoing document: name(s) of principal(s).

Date: _____

_____

Official Signature of Notary

Notary's printed or typed

name, Notary Public

(Official Seal)          My commission expires:

_____

(b)   Repealed by Session Laws 2006-59, s. 19, effective October 1, 2006, and except as otherwise set forth in the act, applicable to notarial acts performed on or after October 1, 2006.

(c)   The notary's printed or typed name as shown in the form provided in subsection (a) of this section is not required if the legible appearance of the notary's name may be ascertained from the notary's typed or printed name near the notary's signature or from elsewhere in the notarial certificate or from the notary's seal if the name is legible.

§ 10B-42.  Notarial certificate for a verification or of subscribing witness.

(a)   When properly completed by a notary, a notarial certificate in substantially the following form may be used and shall be sufficient under the law of this State to satisfy the requirements for a notarial certificate for the verification or proof of the signature of a principal by a subscribing witness. The authorization of the form in this section does not preclude the use of other forms.

_____ County, North Carolina

I certify that (name of subscribing witness) personally appeared before me this day and certified to me under oath or by affirmation that he or she is not a grantee or beneficiary of the transaction, signed the foregoing document as a subscribing witness, and either (i) witnessed (name of principal) sign the foregoing document or (ii) witnessed (name of principal) acknowledge his or her signature on the already-signed document.

Date: _____          _____

                          Official Signature of Notary
                          Notary's printed or typed
                          name, Notary Public
(Official Seal)           My commission expires:

                          _____

(b)   Repealed by Session Laws 2006-59, s. 20, effective October 1, 2006, except as otherwise set forth in the act, and applicable to notarial acts performed on or after October 1, 2006.

(c)   The notary's printed or typed name as shown in the form provided in subsection (a) of this section is not required if the legible appearance of the notary's name may be ascertained from the notary's typed or printed name near the notary's signature or from elsewhere in the notarial certificate or from the notary's seal if the name is legible.

§ 10B-42.1.  Notarial certificate for a verification of nonsubscribing witness.

(a)   When properly completed by a notary, a notarial certificate in substantially the following form may be used and shall be sufficient under the law of this State to satisfy the requirements for a notarial certificate for the verification or proof of the signature of a principal or subscribing witness by a nonsubscribing witness. The authorization of the form in this section does not preclude the use of other forms.

_____ County, North Carolina

I certify (name of nonsubscribing witness) personally appeared before me this day and certified to me under oath or by affirmation that he or she is not a grantee or beneficiary of the transaction, that (name of nonsubscribing witness) recognizes the signature of (name of the principal or the subscribing witness) and that the signature is genuine.

Date: _____           _____
                              Official Signature of Notary
                              Notary's printed or typed
                              name, Notary Public
(Official Seal)               My commission expires:

                              _____

(b)   The notary's printed or typed name as shown in the form provided in subsection (a) of this section is not required if the legible appearance of the notary's name may be ascertained from the notary's typed or printed name near the notary's signature or from elsewhere in the notarial certificate or from the notary's seal if the name is legible.

§ 10B-43. Notarial certificate for an oath or affirmation.

(a)   When properly completed by a notary, a notarial certificate that substantially complies with either of the following forms may be used and shall be sufficient under the law of this State to satisfy the requirements for a notarial certificate for an oath or affirmation. The authorization of the forms in this section does not preclude the use of other forms.

_____ County, North Carolina
Signed and sworn to before me this day by
(name of principal).
Date: _____                _____
                                Official Signature of Notary
                                Notary's printed or typed
                                name, Notary Public
(Official Seal)                 My commission expires:

                                _____

-OR-

_____ County, North Carolina
Sworn to and subscribed before me this day by
(name of principal).
Date: _____                _____
                                Official Signature of Notary
                                Notary's printed or typed
                                name, Notary Public
(Official Seal)                 My commission expires:

                                _____

(b)   Repealed by Session Laws 2006-59, s. 22, effective
October 1, 2006, except as otherwise set forth in the act, and
applicable to notarial acts performed on or after October 1,
2006.

(c)   The notary's printed or typed name as shown in the
form provided in subsection (a) of this section is not required
if the legible appearance of the notary's name may be ascertained from the notary's typed or printed name near the
notary's signature or from elsewhere in the notarial certificate
or from the notary's seal if the name is legible.

(d)   In either of the forms provided under subsection (a) of
this section all of the following shall apply:

    (1)   The name of the principal may be omitted if the
        name of the principal is located near the jurat, and

the principal who so appeared before the notary is clear from the record itself.

(2) The words "affirmed" or "sworn to or affirmed" may be substituted for the words "sworn to".

## Part 7. Changes in Status.

### § 10B-50. Change of address.

Within 45 days after the change of a notary's residence, business, or any mailing address or telephone number, the notary shall send to the Secretary by fax, e-mail, or certified mail, return receipt requested, a signed notice of the change, giving both old and new addresses or telephone numbers.

### § 10B-51. Change of name.

(a) Within 45 days after the legal change of a notary's name, the notary shall send to the Secretary by fax, e-mail, or certified mail, return receipt requested, a signed notice of the change. The notice shall include both the notary's former name and the notary's new name.

(b) A notary with a new name may continue to use the former name in performing notarial acts until all of the following steps have been completed:

(1) The notary receives a confirmation of Notary's Name Change from the Secretary.

(2) The notary obtains a new seal bearing the new name exactly as that name appears in the confirmation from the Secretary.

(3) The notary appears before the register of deeds to which the commission was delivered within 45 days of the effective date of the change to be duly qualified by taking the general oath of office prescribed in G.S. 11-11 and the oath prescribed for officers in G.S. 11-7 under the new name and

to have the notary public record changed to reflect the new commissioned name.

(c)   Upon completion of the requirements in subsection (b) of this section, the notary shall use the new name.

## § 10B-52. Change of county.

(a)   A notary who has moved to another county in North Carolina remains commissioned until the current commission expires, is not required to obtain a new seal, and may continue to notarize without changing his or her seal.

(b)   When a notary who has moved applies to be recommissioned, if the commission is granted the, Secretary shall issue a notice of recommissioning. The commission applicant shall then do all of the following:

(1)   Obtain a new seal bearing the new county exactly as in the notice of recommissioning.

(2)   Appear before the register of deeds to which the commission was delivered within 45 days of recommissioning, to be duly qualified by taking the general oath of office prescribed in G.S. 11-11 and the oath prescribed for officers in G.S. 11-7 under the new county and to have the notary public record changed to reflect the new county name.

## § 10B-53. Change of both name and county.

Within 45 days after the legal change of a notary's name, and if the notary has also moved to a different county than as last commissioned, the notary shall submit to the Secretary a recommissioning application and fee pursuant to this Chapter. The notary may continue to perform notarial acts under the notary's previous name and seal until all of the following steps have been completed:

(1)   The notary receives a transmittal receipt of reappointment due to name and county change from the Secretary.

(2) The notary obtains a new seal bearing the new name and county exactly as those items appear in the transmittal receipt.

(3) The notary appears before the register of deeds to which the commission was delivered within 45 days of recommissioning to be duly qualified by taking the general oath of office prescribed in G.S. 11-11 and the oath prescribed for officers in G.S. 11-7 under the new name and county and to have the notary public record changed to reflect the new name and county.

## § 10B-54. Resignation.

(a) A notary who resigns the notary's commission shall send to the Secretary by fax, e-mail, or certified mail, return receipt requested, a signed notice indicating the effective date of resignation.

(b) Notaries who cease to reside in or to maintain a regular place of work or business in this State, or who become permanently unable to perform their notarial duties, shall resign their commissions and shall deliver their seals to the Secretary by certified mail, return receipt requested.

## § 10B-55. Disposition of seal; death of notary.

(a) When a notary commission is resigned or revoked, the notary shall deliver the notary's seal to the Secretary within 45 days of the resignation or revocation. Delivery shall be accomplished by certified mail, return receipt requested. The Secretary shall destroy any seal received under this subsection.

(b) A notary whose commission has expired and whose previous commission or application was not revoked or denied by this State, is not required to deliver the seal to the Secretary as provided under subsection (a) of this section if the notary intends to apply to be recommissioned and is recommissioned within three months after the notary's commission expires.

(c) If a notary dies while commissioned or before fulfilling the disposition of seal requirements in this section, the notary's estate shall, as soon as is reasonably practicable and no later than the closing of the estate, notify the Secretary in writing of the notary's death and deliver the notary's seal to the Secretary for destruction. A personal representative who is not a notary does not have to comply with the provisions of this subsection if he or she provides a statement under oath in any enforcement proceeding that he or she was unaware that the decedent was a commissioned notary public at the time of death.

## Part 8. Enforcement, Sanctions, and Remedies.

### § 10B-60. Enforcement and penalties.

(a) The Secretary may issue a warning to a notary or restrict, suspend, or revoke a notarial commission for a violation of this Chapter and on any ground for which an application for a commission may be denied under this Chapter. Any period of restriction, suspension, or revocation shall not extend the expiration date of a commission.

(b) Except as otherwise permitted by law, a person who commits any of the following acts is guilty of a Class 1 misdemeanor:

(1) Holding one's self out to the public as a notary if the person does not have a commission.

(2) Performing a notarial act if the person's commission has expired or been suspended or restricted.

(3) Performing a notarial act before the person had taken the oath of office.

(c) A notary shall be guilty of a Class 1 misdemeanor if the notary does any of the following:

(1) Takes an acknowledgment or administers an oath or affirmation without the principal appearing in person before the notary.

(2) Takes a verification or proof without the subscribing witness appearing in person before the notary.

(3) Takes an acknowledgment or administers an oath or affirmation without personal knowledge or satisfactory evidence of the identity of the principal.

(4) Takes a verification or proof without personal knowledge or satisfactory evidence of the identity of the subscribing witness.

(d) A notary shall be guilty of a Class I felony if the notary does any of the following:

(1) Takes an acknowledgment or a verification or a proof, or administers an oath or affirmation if the notary knows it is false or fraudulent.

(2) Takes an acknowledgment or administers an oath or affirmation without the principal appearing in person before the notary if the notary does so with the intent to commit fraud.

(3) Takes a verification or proof without the subscribing witness appearing in person before the notary if the notary does so with the intent to commit fraud.

(e) It is a Class I felony for any person to perform notarial acts in this State with the knowledge that the person is not commissioned under this Chapter.

(f) Any person who without authority obtains, uses, conceals, defaces, or destroys the seal or notarial records of a notary is guilty of a Class I felony.

(g) For purposes of enforcing this Chapter and Article 34 of Chapter 66 of the General Statutes, the following provisions are applicable:

(1) Law enforcement agents of the Department of the Secretary of State have statewide jurisdiction and have all of the powers and authority of law enforcement officers. The agents have the authority to assist local law enforcement agencies in their investigations and to initiate and carry out, on their own or in coordination with local law enforcement agencies, investigations of violations.

(2) Any party to a transaction requiring a notarial certificate for verification and any attorney licensed in this State who is involved in such a transaction in any capacity, whether or not the attorney is representing one of the parties to the transaction, may execute an affidavit and file it with the Secretary of State, setting forth the actions which the affiant alleges constitute violations. Upon receipt of the affidavit, law enforcement agents of the Department shall initiate and carry out, on their own or in coordination with local law enforcement agencies, investigations of violations.

(h) Resignation or expiration of a notarial commission does not terminate or preclude an investigation into a notary's conduct by the Secretary, who may pursue the investigation to a conclusion, whereupon it may be a matter of public record whether or not the finding would have been grounds for disciplinary action.

(i) The Secretary may seek injunctive relief against any person who violates the provisions of this Chapter. Nothing in this Chapter diminishes the authority of the North Carolina State Bar.

(j) Any person who knowingly solicits, coerces, or in any material way influences a notary to commit official misconduct, is guilty as an aider and abettor and is subject to the same level of punishment as the notary.

(k)   The sanctions and remedies of this Chapter supplement other sanctions and remedies provided by law, including, but not limited to, forgery and aiding and abetting.

(l)   The Secretary shall notify the North Carolina State Bar (State Bar) of any final decision finding a violation of subsection (a) of this section by a notary who is also an attorney-at-law licensed under Chapter 84 of the General Statutes. The Secretary shall endeavor to provide a copy of any court order rendered under subsection (b), (c), (d), (e), (f), or (j) of this section to the State Bar in cases where the notary is an attorney-at-law licensed under Chapter 84 of the General Statutes. Any referral by the Secretary to the State Bar under this subsection shall be considered a showing of professional unfitness under G.S. 84-28(d), and the State Bar shall administer discipline accordingly.

## Part 9. Validation of Notarial Acts.

§ 10B-65.  Acts of notaries public in certain instances validated.

(a)   Any acknowledgment taken and any instrument notarized by a person prior to qualification as a notary public but after commissioning or recommissioning as a notary public, or by a person whose notary commission has expired, is hereby validated. The acknowledgment and instrument shall have the same legal effect as if the person qualified as a notary public at the time the person performed the act.

(b)   All documents bearing a notarial seal and which contain any of the following errors are validated and given the same legal effect as if the errors had not occurred:

    (1)   The date of the expiration of the notary's commission is stated, whether correctly or erroneously.

(2) The notarial seal does not contain a readable impression of the notary's name, contains an incorrect spelling of the notary's name, or does not bear the name of the notary exactly as it appears on the commission, as required under G.S. 10B-37.

(3) The notary's signature does not comport exactly with the name on the notary commission or on the notary seal, as required by G.S. 10B-20.

(4) The notarial seal contains typed, printed, drawn, or handwritten material added to the seal, fails to contain the words "North Carolina" or the abbreviation "NC", or contains correct information except that instead of the abbreviation for North Carolina contains the abbreviation for another state.

(5) The date of the acknowledgement, the verification or proof, or the oath or affirmation states the correct day and month but lacks a year or states an incorrect year.

(c) All deeds of trust in which the notary was named in the document as a trustee only are validated.

(d) All notary acknowledgments performed before December 1, 2005, bearing a notarial seal are hereby validated.

(e) This section applies to notarial acts performed on or before April 1, 2013.

§ 10B-66. Certain notarial acts validated.

(a) Any acknowledgment taken and any instrument notarized by a person whose notarial commission was revoked on or before January 30, 1997, is hereby validated.

(b) This section applies to notarial acts performed on or before August 1, 1998.

## § 10B-67. Erroneous commission expiration date cured.

An erroneous statement of the date that the notary's commission expires shall not affect the sufficiency, validity, or enforceability of the notarial certificate or the related record if the notary is, in fact, lawfully commissioned at the time of the notarial act. This section applies to notarial acts whenever performed.

## § 10B-68. Technical defects cured.

(a)   Technical defects, errors, or omissions in a notarial certificate shall not affect the sufficiency, validity, or enforceability of the notarial certificate or the related instrument or document.

(b)   Defects in the commissioning or recommissioning of a notary that are approved by the Department are cured. This subsection applies to commissions and recommissions issued on or after December 1, 2005.

(c)   As used in this section, a technical defect includes those cured under G.S. 10B-37(f) and G.S. 10B-67. Other technical defects include, but are not limited to, the absence of the legible appearance of the notary's name exactly as shown on the notary's commission as required in G.S. 10B-20(b), the affixation of the notary's seal near the signature of the principal or subscribing witness rather than near the notary's signature, minor typographical mistakes in the spelling of the principal's name, the failure to acknowledge the principal's name exactly as signed by including or omitting initials, or the failure to specify the principal's title or office, if any.

## § 10B-69. Official forms cured.

(a)   The notarial certificate contained in a form issued by a State agency prior to April 1, 2013, is deemed to be a valid certificate provided the certificate complied with the law at the time the form was issued.

(b)   The notarization using a certificate under subsection (a) of this section shall be deemed valid if executed in compliance with the law at the time the form was issued.

## § 10B-70. Certain notarial acts for local government agencies validated.

(a)  Any acknowledgment taken and any instrument notarized for a local government agency by a person prior to qualification as a notary public but after commissioning or recommissioning as a notary public, by a person whose notary commission has expired, or by a person who failed to qualify within 45 days of commissioning as required by G.S. 10B-10, is hereby validated. The acknowledgment and instrument shall have the same legal effect as if the person qualified as a notary public at the time the person performed the act. This section shall apply to notarial acts performed for a local government agency on or after October 31, 2006, and before June 30, 2007.

(b)  Any electronic document filed in the Mecklenburg County Register of Deeds office that purports to be notarized in the Commonwealth of Virginia and that contains the typed name of a Virginia notary together with the notary's expiration date shall be given the same legal effect as if the person performed a lawful notarization in Virginia.

## § 10B-71. Certain notarial acts validated when recommissioned notary failed to again take oath.

Any acknowledgment taken and any instrument notarized by a person who after recommissioning failed to again take the oath as a notary public is hereby validated. The acknowledgment and instrument shall have the same legal effect as if the person qualified as a notary public at the time the person performed the act. This section shall apply to notarial acts performed on or after May 15, 2004, and before April 1, 2013.

## § 10B-72. Certain notarial acts validated when recommissioned notary failed to again take oath.

Any acknowledgment taken and any instrument notarized by a person who after recommissioning failed to again take the oath as a notary public is hereby validated. The acknowledgment and instrument shall have the same legal effect as if the person qualified as a notary public at the time the person performed the act. This section shall apply to notarial acts performed on or after August 28, 2010, and before January 12, 2012.

§ 10B-99. Presumption of regularity.

(a)  In the absence of evidence of fraud on the part of the notary, or evidence of a knowing and deliberate violation of this Article by the notary, the courts shall grant a presumption of regularity to notarial acts so that those acts may be upheld, provided there has been substantial compliance with the law. Nothing in this Chapter modifies or repeals the common law doctrine of substantial compliance in effect on November 30, 2005.

(b)  A notarial act shall be deemed valid if it complies with the law as it existed on or before December 1, 2005. This section applies to notarial acts whenever performed.

# Appendix B: North Carolina Administrative Code

TITLE 18—SECRETARY OF STATE

CHAPTER 07—NOTARY PUBLIC DIVISION

SUBCHAPTER B—NOTARY PUBLIC SECTION

SECTION .0100—GENERAL PROVISIONS

18 NCAC 07B .0101  SCOPE
The rules in this Subchapter implement Chapter 10B of the General Statutes, the Notary Public and Electronic Notary Acts. The rules govern the qualification, commissioning, notarial acts, conduct and discipline of notaries as Constitutional officers of the State.

18 NCAC 07B .0102  DEFINITIONS
(a)  The definitions in G.S. 10B-3 apply to this Subchapter.
(b)  For purposes of Chapter 10B of the General Statutes and Subchapters 07B and 07C of this Chapter:
    (1)  "Applicant" means an individual who seeks appointment or reappointment to the office of notary public;
    (2)  "Appoint" or "Appointment" means the naming of an individual to the office of notary public after determination that the individual has complied with Chapter 10B of the General Statutes and Subchapter 07B of this Chapter. For the purposes of these Rules,

the terms "appoint", "reappoint", "appointment", "reappointment", "commission", "recommission", "commissioning", and "recommissioning" all refer to the term "commission" as defined in G.S. 10B-3(4) or to the process of acquiring or maintaining such commission;

(3) "Appointee" means an individual who has been appointed or reappointed to the office of notary public but has not yet taken the oath of office to be commissioned;

(4) "Commissioning date" means the date of commissioning or recommissioning as entered on a commission certificate;

(5) "Crime" means a crime or:
   (A) Attempt to commit a crime;
   (B) Accessory to commission of a crime;
   (C) Aiding and abetting of a crime;
   (D) Conspiracy to commit a crime; or
   (E) Solicitation to commit a crime.

(6) "Division" means the Notary Public Section of the North Carolina Department of the Secretary of State.

## 18 NCAC 07B .0103 LOCATION, HOURS AND CONTACT INFORMATION

(a) Mailing Address. The mailing address for the Division of Certification and Filing, Notary Public Section is P.O. Box 29626, Raleigh, NC 27626-0626.

(b) Hours. Office hours for the public are 8:00 a.m. to 4:00 p.m. Monday through Friday with the exception of state holidays.

(c) Contacting the Division. In addition to contacting the Division by mail as provided in Paragraph (a) of this Rule, contact with the Division may be by:

(1) On-line information service: The Department provides on-line information services at its website: www.sosnc.com.

(2)  Electronic Mail: For basic information the Notary Public Section may be contacted by email at notary@sosnc.com. Electronic mail shall not be used for filing applications.

(3)  Telephone Number: The telephone number for Notary Customer Service is (919) 807-2219.

(4)  Fax Number: To send information to the Notary Public Section via fax, the number is (919) 807-2210.

## 18 NCAC 07B .0104   FORMS

All forms issued pursuant to Chapter 10B of the General Statutes may be found on the Department's website or may be obtained by contacting the Department using one of the means set out in Rule .0103 of this Subchapter.

## 18 NCAC 07B .0105   FEES

(a)  Fees shall be paid by a personal or business check, a money order, or a cashier's check in U.S. dollars and cents made payable to the N.C. Department of the Secretary of State.

(b)  Fees for on-line applications may be paid by an auto-mated clearinghouse debit account (ACH).

(c)  If a fee is paid with a check or other instrument which is returned by the institution upon which it was issued for "insufficient funds" or for other similar reason:

(1)  The Division shall issue a notice of intent to deny the application or revoke the commission; and

(2)  The Division shall issue a denial or revocation if the fee is not paid in full within 10 business days after the date on the notice of intent to deny or revoke.

(3)  The Division shall charge a twenty-five dollar ($25.00) fee for which payment has been refused by the payor's bank for insufficient funds or for no account.

## 18 NCAC 07B .0106 WAIVER

The Director may waive any rule in this Subchapter that is not statutorily required based on the factors set forth in Rule .0901 of this Chapter.

## 18 NCAC 07B .0107 CONTINUING OBLIGATIONS OF NOTARIES

(a) A notary shall notify the Director of changes in name, address or county as required by G.S. 10B-50, 10B-51, and 10B-53.

(b) A notary shall notify the Director that the notary has been convicted of a crime as set out in G.S. 10B-3(9) and Rule .0201 of this Subchapter, within 45 days of the date on which judgment is entered.

(c) A notary shall notify the Director of changes in:

(1) Residency or place of work to a location outside the State of North Carolina;

(2) Residency status in the United States;

(3) Ability to speak, read and write the English language;

(4) A finding or admission of liability in a civil lawsuit based upon the notary's deceit;

(5) Revocation, suspension, restriction, or denial of a professional license by the State of North Carolina or any other state or nation;

(6) A finding that the notary has engaged in official misconduct, whether or not disciplinary action resulted;

(7) A finding or a charge that a notary has knowingly used false or misleading advertising in which the notary was represented as having powers, duties, rights or privileges that a North Carolina notary, by law, does not possess; or

(8) The North Carolina State Bar or the courts of North Carolina or the bar or courts of any other state or

nation finding that the notary has engaged in the unauthorized practice of law.

(d) A notary shall respond within the time period set out in a request from the Director for information, including a request for information regarding wrongful notarial acts alleged to have been performed by the notary.

## SECTION .0200—APPLICATIONS

18 NCAC 07B .0201  GENERAL

(a)  Other Professional Licenses. An applicant shall list on his or her application all suspensions, revocations and other disciplinary actions taken against the applicant regarding the applicant's current or former professional licenses.

(b)  Criminal Record. An applicant shall list on his or her application all misdemeanor and felony convictions related to crimes of dishonesty and moral turpitude. For purposes of this Chapter, those crimes include:

(1) Arson;
(2) Assault;
(3) Battery;
(4) Burglary;
(5) Carrying a concealed weapon without a permit;
(6) Child molestation;
(7) Child pornography;
(8) Discharge of a firearm in a public place or into a dwelling;
(9) Domestic violence;
(10) Driving under the influence;
(11) Unlawful possession or sale of drugs;
(12) Embezzlement;
(13) Failure to comply with a court order;
(14) Failure to pay child support;

(15) Failure to return to confinement;

(16) False financial statements;

(17) Forgery;

(18) Fraud;

(19) Identity theft;

(20) Impersonation of a law enforcement officer;

(21) Hit and run;

(22) Kidnapping;

(23) Prostitutions;

(24) Multiple worthless checks showing a pattern of behavior indicating moral turpitude and dishonesty;

(25) A worthless check in excess of five hundred dollars ($500.00);

(26) Possession of an unregistered firearm;

(27) Practicing law without a license;

(28) Rape;

(29) Receipt of stolen goods or property;

(30) Resisting arrest;

(31) Robbery;

(32) Statutory rape;

(33) Tax evasion;

(34) Terrorist threats or acts;

(35) Theft;

(36) Threats to commit a crime or cause bodily injury;

(37) Spousal abuse.

(c)   In considering whether to appoint or reappoint an applicant to the office of notary public, the Director may consider the factors set forth in Rule .0901 of this Subchapter.

## SECTION .0300—INITIAL APPOINTMENT

18 NCAC 07B .0301   INITIAL COMMISSION

(a)   Application Form.

(1) Applicants for initial appointment shall use the application form designated by the Division for that purpose and may download the application form from the Department's website.

(2) Applicants for initial appointment who are members of the North Carolina State Bar may download the application form from the Department's website and may file the completed application without first obtaining a signature from a notary instructor.

(3) All other applicants for initial appointment who download the application form from the Department's website shall obtain a signature on the application from a notary instructor certifying that the applicant successfully completed the required course of instruction before the applicant may file the form with the Department.

(b) Submission of Application. An applicant for an initial appointment shall submit his or her application by:

(1) U.S. mail;

(2) In person delivery; or

(3) Courier service.

## 18 NCAC 07B .0302 TIMING OF FILING OF INITIAL APPLICATION

(a) Submission deadline. An applicant for initial appointment who is not a licensed member of the North Carolina State Bar shall submit an application within three months after passing the examination required by G.S. 10B-8.

(b) An applicant who applies more than three months after compliance with G.S. 10B-8(a) shall

(1) Comply again with G.S. 10B-8(a);

(2) Submit an application for initial appointment; and

(3) Pay the application fee.

# SECTION .0400—REAPPOINTMENT OF NOTARIES PUBLIC

## 18 NCAC 07B .0401   REAPPOINTMENT

(a)   Application for Reappointment.

    (1)   An applicant for reappointment shall submit an application for reappointment.

    (2)   Applicants for reappointment may apply on-line on the Department's website.

(b)   Timing of Application for Reappointment. An applicant for reappointment shall apply for reappointment no earlier than 10 weeks before the expiration date of the applicant's commission.

## 18 NCAC 07B .0402   REAPPOINTMENT TEST

(a)   Attorneys who are licensed members of the North Carolina State Bar do not have to take a reappointment test.

(b)   The reappointment test may be taken either:

    (1)   By completing the on-line test on the Department's website;

    (2)   By completing a paper test at the Department's offices at a time based upon:

        (A)   The availability of the Division's staff; and

        (B)   The availability of the applicant; or

    (3)   By completing a paper test at a time and place mutually agreed upon by the applicant and a certified notary public instructor.

(c)   An applicant for reappointment shall have 30 minutes to complete the test. An applicant needing accommodation pursuant to the Americans with Disabilities Act shall contact the Division and request the accommodation.

(d)   If an applicant fails the reappointment test, the applicant may re-take the test no more than two times within 30 days of the date on which the test is first taken.

(e) If the applicant fails to pass the reappointment test within 30 days, the applicant shall not be reappointed and the application shall be denied.

## 18 NCAC 07B .0403 APPLICATION AFTER REAPPOINTMENT DENIAL BASED ON FAILING TEST

An applicant for reappointment whose application is denied due to failure to pass the reappointment test may reapply by:

(1) Complying with G.S. 10B-8(a);

(2) Submitting an application for reappointment; and

(3) Paying the application fee.

## SECTION .0500—COMMISSIONS

## 18 NCAC 07B .0501 APPOINTMENT AND ISSUANCE OF COMMISSIONING CERTIFICATE

(a) Upon determination that an applicant has complied with all requirements of the Act and this Subchapter, the Director shall appoint or reappoint the applicant to the office of notary public and issue a commissioning certificate.

(b) The Division shall send the commissioning certificate to the Register of Deeds in the county of commissioning.

(c) The Division shall send the appointee notice that:

(1) The commissioning certificate has been issued; and

(2) The appointee shall appear within 45 days of the commissioning date to take the oath of office before the Register of Deeds in the county of commissioning.

## 18 NCAC 07B .0502 COMMISSIONING CERTIFICATE DATE

(a) A commissioning certificate shall not be back-dated.

(b) Applications shall not be deemed received until complete.

## 18 NCAC 07B .0503   OATH OF OFFICE AND DELIVERY OF COMMISSIONING CERTIFICATE

(a)   Before taking the oath of office, an appointee shall present to the Register of Deeds satisfactory evidence of the appointee's identity as set out in G.S. 10B-3(22).

(b)   The Register of Deeds shall document the type of evidence provided by the appointee on the form provided by the Department.

(c)   After administering the oath of office the Register of Deeds shall deliver the commissioning certificate to the notary public.

## 18 NCAC 07B .0504   REAPPOINTMENT IF OATH NOT TAKEN WITHIN 45 DAYS

(a)   An appointee who fails to take the oath of office within 45 days of the commissioning certificate date may reapply for reappointment.

(b)   Reapplication within one year of commission date. If an appointee seeks reappointment more than 45 days and less than one year after the commissioning certificate date, the appointee shall:

    (1)   Apply for reappointment;

    (2)   Submit another application fee; and

    (3)   Pass the reappointment test.

(c)   Reapplication one year or more after commissioning certificate date. If an appointee seeks reappointment one year or more after the commissioning certificate date, the appointee shall:

    (1)   Comply with the requirements of G.S. 10B-8(a);

    (2)   Apply for reappointment; and

    (3)   Submit another application fee.

## 18 NCAC 07B .0505   TERM OF OFFICE

(a)   A notary's commission or recommission shall not be effective until the oath of office has been administered.

(b)    A notary's five year term of office begins on the date on the commissioning certificate.

. . . .

## SECTION .0900—ENFORCEMENT AND DISCIPLINARY ACTION

**18 NCAC 07B .0901    FACTORS CONSIDERED IN DISCIPLINARY ACTIONS**

When determining whether to deny an application or take disciplinary action against a notary, the Director may consider a variety of factors including:

(1)    Nature, number and severity of any acts, offenses, official misconduct or crimes under consideration;

(2)    Evidence pertaining to the honesty, credibility, truthfulness, and integrity of the applicant or notary public;

(3)    Actual or potential monetary or other harm to the general public, group, individual, or client;

(4)    History of complaints received by the Department;

(5)    Prior disciplinary record or warning from the Department;

(6)    Evidence in mitigation;

(7)    Evidence in aggravation;

(8)    Occupational, vocational, or professional license disciplinary record;

(9)    Evidence of rehabilitation. NOTE: Examples include reference letters and proof of class attendance;

(10)    Criminal record;

(11)    Reports from law enforcement agencies;

(12)    Willfulness;

(13)    Negligence.

## 18 NCAC 07B .0902 GENERAL APPLICATION DENIAL

(a) Unqualified applicant. The Director shall deny the application of an applicant for a notary public commission who does not qualify for office based on the factors set forth in Chapter 10B of the General Statutes and this Subchapter.

(b) Current disciplinary action. The Director shall deny an application if the application is submitted before the expiration of a period of suspension or revocation of a commission previously held by the applicant.

(c) Information regarding convictions and judgments.

    (1) The Director shall deny an application which contains false information about the applicant's criminal record or record of civil lawsuit findings or admissions of liability based on the applicant's deceit; or

    (2) The Director may deny an application which contains misleading information, including:

        (A) The applicant's criminal record, including whether all charges were dismissed or consolidated or whether all terms and conditions of a judgment have been completed;

        (B) Misstatement or omission of a nonmaterial fact;

        (C) Whether a civil lawsuit included findings based on the applicant's deceit; or

        (D) Whether, in a civil lawsuit or settlement of a civil lawsuit, an applicant made admissions of liability related to the applicant's deceit.

(d) Applicant notarization. The Director shall deny an application if the applicant notarizes his or her own signature.

(e) The Director shall deny an application if the applicant:

    (1) Leaves three or more sections of the application incomplete;

    (2) Fails to submit an application for initial appointment within 90 days of class; or

(3)   Fails to submit complete and correct information on an application for initial appointment or reappointment after three submissions by the applicant.

## 18 NCAC 07B .0903   EXECUTED DOCUMENT VIOLATIONS

The Director shall revoke the commission of a notary who performs a notarial act knowing that the document or information contained in it is false or fraudulent, or that the intent of the executed document is dishonest. Acts of fraud or dishonesty include:

(1)   Notarizing a blank DMV vehicle title document;
(2)   Embezzlement;
(3)   Forgery;
(4)   Fraud;
(5)   Identity theft;
(6)   Impersonation of a law enforcement officer;
(7)   Receiving stolen goods or property; and
(8)   Theft.

## 18 NCAC 07B .0904   COMPLETE AND LAWFUL NOTARIAL ACT VIOLATIONS

(a)   The Director may take disciplinary action against a notary for an offense relating to failure to meet the statutory requirements for a notarial act.

(b)   Offenses relating to failure to meet the statutory requirements for a complete and lawful notarial act include:

(1)   Incomplete attestation;
(2)   Improper acknowledgment language;
(3)   Incorrect signature;
(4)   Incorrect expiration date;
(5)   Failure to administer an oath or affirmation;
(6)   Failure to verify identification;
(7)   Failure to require personal appearance;
(8)   Notarization of a document in which the notary is a named, interested, or signed party;

(9) Notarization of a "non-signature" or a copy of a signature;

(10) Charging a fee in excess of that which is set by law, including fees for mileage or travel;

(11) Acting as a notary when not commissioned;

(12) Unauthorized use of a seal.

## 18 NCAC 07B .0905   OTHER VIOLATIONS

The Director may take disciplinary action against a notary for violation of Chapter 10B of the General Statutes or this Subchapter, including failure to provide information required by Rule .0107 of this Subchapter.

## 18 NCAC 07B .0906   MINIMUM SANCTION

(a) If a notary commits a combination of acts of official misconduct, the notary shall receive, at a minimum, the maximum penalty of the lesser of the acts committed.

(b) Nothing in this Section shall restrict the Secretary from using any other statutory penalty available.

## 18 NCAC 07B .0907   APPEAL PROCEDURES

(a) Applicants for commissioning or recommissioning whose applications have been denied and notaries who have received disciplinary action by the Director have the right to file a petition for a contested case hearing pursuant to Article 3 of Chapter 150B of the General Statutes.

(b) Petition forms may be obtained from the Office of Administrative Hearings, 424 North Blount Street, 6714 Mail Service Center, Raleigh, NC 27699-6714; (919) 733-2698; http://www.oah.state.nc.us/.

(c) A copy of a Petition filed with the Office of Administrative Hearings must also be served on the process agent for the Department of the Secretary of State.

# SECTION .1000—PUBLIC RECORDS AND REQUESTS FOR INFORMATION

**18 NCAC 07B .1001   PUBLIC INFORMATION**

(a)   The information that the Department shall make available on individual notaries public include:

   (1)   Full legal name;

   (2)   County of Commission;

   (3)   Employer's Name;

   (4)   Employer's street and mailing addresses;

   (5)   Employer's phone number;

   (6)   Status of Commission;

   (7)   Disciplinary action, if any.

(b)   A request for confidential notary information shall be in writing and shall include documentation of the right of the requestor to receive the confidential notary information, including:

   (1)   Authorization of the notary that the person is an agent of the notary authorized to request and receive the information;

   (2)   Subpoena or court order;

   (3)   Statement of authority from a law enforcement or government agency; or

   (4)   N.C. State Bar applicant "Release of Information" form.

# Appendix C: North Carolina Registers of Deeds Contact Information

**Alamance**

PO Box 837
118 W. Harden St.
Graham, NC 27253-0837
336.570.6565
www.alamance-nc.com

**Alexander**

75 1st St. SW, Ste. 1
Taylorsville, NC 28681
828.632.3152
www.alexandercountync.gov

**Alleghany**

PO Box 186
348 S. Main St.
Courthouse
Sparta, NC 28675
336.372.4342
www.alleghanycounty-nc.gov

**Anson**

PO Box 352
101 S. Greene St.
Ste. 131
Wadesboro, NC 28170
704.994.3208
www.co.anson.nc.us

**Ashe**

150 Government Cir.
Ste. 2300
Jefferson, NC 28640
336.846.5580
www.ashencrod.org

**Avery**

PO Box 87
200 Montezuma St.
Courthouse
Newland, NC 28657
828.733.8260
www.averydeeds.com

**Beaufort**

PO Box 514
112 W. 2nd St.
Washington, NC 27889
252.946.2323
www.beaufortcountyrod.com

**Bertie**

PO Box 340
108 Dundee St.
Courthouse
Windsor, NC 27983
252.794.5309
www.co.bertie.nc.us

## Bladen

PO Box 247
Elizabethtown, NC 28337
910.862.6710
www.bladeninfo.com

## Brunswick

PO Box 87
75 Courthouse Dr.
Bolivia, NC 28422
910.253.2690
rod.brunsco.net

## Buncombe

205 College St.
Asheville, NC 28801
828.250.4300
www.buncombecounty.org

## Burke

201 S. Green St.
PO Box 219
Morganton, NC 28680
828.438.5451
rod.burkenc.org

## Cabarrus

PO Box 707
65 Church St., SE
Concord, NC 28026
704.920.2112
www.cabarrusncrod.org

## Caldwell

905 West Ave., NW
County Office Bldg.
Lenoir, NC 28645
828.757.1310
www.caldwellrod.org

## Camden

PO Box 190
117 N. 343
Camden, NC 27921
252.338.1919, Ext. 244
www.camdencountync.gov

## Carteret

302 Courthouse Square
Administration Bldg.
Beaufort, NC 28516
252.728.8474
www.carteretcountync.gov

## Caswell

PO Box 98
139 E. Church St.
Yanceyville, NC 27379
336.694.4197
www.caswellcountync.gov

## Catawba

PO Box 65
100 SW Blvd., Bldg. B
Newton, NC 28658
828.465.1573
www.catawbacountync.gov

## Chatham

PO Box 756
Courthouse Annex
Courthouse Cir.
Pittsboro, NC 27312
919.542.8235
www.chathamncrod.org

## Cherokee

53 Peachtree St.
Murphy, NC 28906
828.837.2613
www.cherokeencrod.org

## Chowan

PO Box 487
101 S. Broad St.
Courthouse
Edenton, NC 27932
252.482.2619
www.chowancounty-nc.gov

## Clay

PO Box 118
261 Courthouse Dr.
Hayesville, NC 28904
828.389.0087
www.clayconc.com

## Cleveland

PO Box 1210
311 E. Marion St.
Shelby, NC 28150
704.484.4834
www.clevelandrod.com

## Columbus

PO Box 1086
125 Washington St., Ste. B
Whiteville, NC 28472
910.640.6625
www.columbusdeeds.com

## Craven

226 Pollock St.
New Bern, NC 28560
252.636.6617
www.cravencounty.com

## Cumberland

PO Box 2039
117 Dick St.
Rm. 114
Fayetteville, NC 28301
910.678.7775
www.ccrod.org

## Currituck

PO Box 71
2801 Caratoke Hwy.
Ste. 300
Currituck, NC 27929
252.232.3297
www.co.currituck.nc.us

## Dare

PO Box 70
Dare Co. Justice Center
962 Marshall Collins Dr.
Manteo, NC 27954
252.475.5970
www.darenc.com

## Davidson

PO Box 464
203 W. Second St.
Lexington, NC 27292
336.242.2150
www.co.davidson.nc.us

## Davie

123 S. Main St.
Mocksville, NC 27028
336.753.6080
www.daviencrod.org

## Duplin

PO Box 970
118 Duplin St., Rm. # 106
Kenansville, NC 28349
910.296.2108
www.duplinrod.com

## Durham

PO Box 1107
200 E. Main St.
Durham, NC 27701
919.560.0480
dconc.gov

## Edgecombe

PO Box 386
301 St. Andrews St.
Tarboro, NC 27886
252.641.7928
www.edgecombecountync.gov

## Forsyth

PO Box 20639
201 N. Chestnut St.
Winston-Salem, NC 27101
336.703.2700
www.co.forsyth.nc.us

## Franklin

PO Box 545
113 S. Main St.
Louisburg, NC 27549
919.496.3500
www.franklincountync.us

## Gaston

PO Box 1578
325 N. Marietta St.
Gastonia, NC 28053
704.862.7680
www.gastongov.com

## Gates

PO Box 471
202 Court St.
Gatesville, NC 27938
252.357.0850
www.gatesrod.net

## Graham

PO Box 406
12 N. Main St.
Robbinsville, NC 28771
828.479.7971
www.grahamcounty.org

## Granville

PO Box 427
101 Main St.
Courthouse
Oxford, NC 27565
919.693.6314
www.granvillecounty.org

## Greene

PO Box 86
301 N. Greene St.
Snow Hill, NC 28580
252.747.3620
www.co.greene.nc.us

## Guilford

PO Box 3427
201 S. Eugene St.
Greensboro, NC 27402
336.641.7556
336.641.3690
www.myguilford.com

## Halifax

PO Box 67
357 Ferrell Ln.
Halifax, NC 27839
252.583.2101
www.halifaxnc.com

## Harnett

PO Box 279
305 W. Cornelius Harnett Blvd.,
Ste. 200
Lillington, NC 27546
910.893.7540
www.harnett.org

## Haywood

215 N. Main St.
Courthouse Ste. 213
Waynesville, NC 28786
828.452.6635
www.haywooddeeds.com

## Henderson

200 N. Grove St., Ste. 129
Hendersonville, NC 28792
828.697.4901
www.hendersoncountync.org

## Hertford

119 Justice Dr., Ste. 9
Winton, NC 27986
252.358.7850
www.hertfordrod.net

## Hoke

113 Campus Ave.
Raeford, NC 28376
910.875.2035
www.hokencrod.org

## Hyde

PO Box 294
30 Oyster Creek Rd.
Swan Quarter, NC 27885
252.926.4181
www.hyderod.net

## Iredell

Hall of Justice Annex
201 E. Water St.
Statesville, NC 28687
704.872.7468
www.co.iredell.nc.us

## Jackson

401 Grindstaff Cove Rd.
Ste. 108
Jackson Co. Justice Center
Sylva, NC 28779
828.586.7535
www.jacksonnc.org

## Johnston

PO Box 118
207 E. Johnston St.
Office Ste. 209
Smithfield, NC 27577
919.989.5160
www.johnstonnc.com

## Jones

PO Box 189
101 Market St.
Courthouse
Trenton, NC 28585
252.448.2551
www.jonescountync.gov

## Lee

PO Box 2040
1408 S. Horner Blvd.
Sanford, NC 27331
919.718.4585
www.leencrod.org

## Lenoir

PO Box 3289
101 N. Queen St.
Kinston, NC 28502
252.559.6420
www.co.lenoir.nc.us

## Lincoln

105-A E. Court Square, 2nd Floor
Lincolnton, NC 28092
704.736.8534
www.lincolncounty.org

## Macon

5 W. Main St.
Courthouse
Franklin, NC 28734
828.349.2095
www.maconncdeeds.com

## Madison

PO Box 66
2 N. Main St.
Courthouse
Marshall, NC 28753
828.649.3131
www.madisonrod.net

## Martin

PO Box 348
305 E. Main St.
Martin Co. Governmental Center
Williamston, NC 27892
252.789.4320
www.martincountyncgov.com

## McDowell

21 S. Main St., Ste. A
Marion, NC 28752
828.652.4727
www.mcdowellgov.com

## Mecklenburg

720 E. 4th St., Rm. 103
Charlotte, NC 28202
704.336.2443
www.mecklenburgcountync.gov

## Mitchell

PO Box 82
26 Crimson Laurel Cir.
Ste. 4
Bakersville, NC 28705
828.688.2139
www.mitchelldeeds.com

## Montgomery

PO Box 695
102 E. Spring St.
Troy, NC 27371
910.576.4271
www.montgomeryrod.net

## Moore

PO Box 1210
100 Dowd St.
Carthage, NC 28327
910.947.6370
moorecountync.gov

## Nash

PO Box 974
120 W. Washington St.
Nashville, NC 27856
252.459.9836
www.co.nash.nc.us

## New Hanover

216 North 2nd St.
Wilmington, NC 28401
910.798.4530
registerofdeeds.nhcgov.com

## Northampton

PO Box 128
104 Thomas Bragg St.
Jackson, NC 27845
252.534.2511
www.northamptonnc.com

## Onslow

109 Old Bridge St. Rm. 107
Jacksonville, NC 28540
910.347.3451
www.onslowcountync.gov/register

## Orange

PO Box 8181
Gateway Center
228 S. Churton St., Ste. 300
Hillsborough, NC 27278
919.245.2675
www.orangecountync.gov

## Pamlico

PO Box 433
202 Main St.
Courthouse Square
Bayboro, NC 28515
252.745.4421
www.pamlicocounty.org

## Pasquotank

PO Box 154
206 E. Main St.
Elizabeth City, NC 27909
252.335.4367
www.pasquotankrod.net

## Pender

PO Box 43
300 E. Fremont St.
Burgaw, NC 28425
910.259.1205
www.pendercountync.gov

## Perquimans

PO Box 74
128 N. Church St.
Hertford, NC 27944
252.426.5660
www.perquimansrod.us

## Person

PO Box 209
21 Abbitt St.
Roxboro, NC 27573
336.597.1733
www.personrod.net

## Pitt

Pitt County Courthouse
PO Box 35
100 West 3rd St.
Greenville, NC 27835
252.902.1650
www.pittcountync.gov

## Polk

PO Box 308
40 Courthouse St.
Columbus, NC 28722
828.894.8450
www.polknc.org

## Randolph

PO Box 4458
158 Worth St.
Asheboro, NC 27204
336.318.6960
www.randrod.com

## Richmond

114 E. Franklin St., Rm. 101
Rockingham, NC 28379
910.997.8250
richmondrod.net

## Robeson

PO Box 22
500 N. Elm St.
Rm. 102
Lumberton, NC 28358
910.671.3044
www.rod.co.robeson.nc.us

## Rockingham

PO Box 56
Courthouse, Ste. 99
1086 NC 65
Wentworth, NC 27375
336.342.8820
www.registerofdeeds.info

## Rowan

PO Box 2568
402 N. Main St.
Salisbury, NC 28144
704.216.8626
www.co.rowan.nc.us

## Rutherford

PO Box 551
229 N. Main St.
Rutherfordton, NC 28139
828.287.6156
rutherfordcountync.gov

## Sampson

101 E. Main St.
Ste. 107
Clinton, NC 28328
910.592.8026
www.sampsonrod.org

## Scotland

PO Box 769
212 Biggs St., Rm. 250
Laurinburg, NC 28352
910.277.2575
www.scotlandcounty.org

## Stanly

PO Box 97
201 S. Second St.
Albemarle, NC 28001
704.986.3640
www.stanlyrod.net

## Stokes

PO Box 67
1014 Main St.
Danbury, NC 27016
336.593.2811
www.stokescorod.org

## Surry

PO Box 303
201 E. Kapp St
Dobson, NC 27017
336.401.8150
www.co.surry.nc.us

## Swain

PO Box 1183
101 Mitchell St.
Bryson City, NC 28713
828.488.9273
www.swaincorod.org

## Transylvania

7 E. Main St.
Brevard, NC 28712
828.884.3162
www.transylvaniadeeds.com

**Tyrrell**

PO Box 449
403 Main St.
Columbia, NC 27925
252.796.2901
www.tyrrellrod.net

**Union**

PO Box 248
500 N. Main St., Rm. 205
Monroe, NC 28112
704.283.3794
www.unionconcrod.org

**Vance**

122 Young St., Ste. F
Henderson, NC 27536
252.738.2110
www.vancecounty.org

**Wake**

PO Box 1897
One Bank of America Plaza
421 Fayetteville St., Ste. 300
Raleigh, NC 27601
919.856.5460
www.wakegov.com

**Warren**

PO Box 506
109 S. Main St.
Courthouse
Warrenton, NC 27589
252.257.3265
www.warrencountync.com

**Washington**

PO Box 1007
120 Adams St.
Plymouth, NC 27962
252.793.2325
www.washingtonrod.net

**Watauga**

842 W. King St.
Courthouse, Ste. 9
Boone, NC 28607
828.265.8052
www.wataugacounty.org

**Wayne**

224-226 E. Walnut St.
Goldsboro, NC 27533
919.731.1449
www.waynegov.com

**Wilkes**

500 Courthouse Dr.
Ste. 1000
Wilkesboro, NC 28697
336.651.7351
www.wilkescounty.net

**Wilson**

PO Box 1728
101 N. Goldsboro St.
Wilson, NC 27894
252.399.2935
www.wilson-co.com

## Yadkin

PO Box 211
101 S. State St.
Yadkinville, NC 27055
336.679.4225
www.yadkincorod.org

## Yancey

110 Town Square Rm. 4
Burnsville, NC 28714
828.682.2174
yanceycountync.gov/register-of-deeds